Cross Stitch
Greeting Cards

Cross Stitch Greeting Cards

OVER 50 DESIGNS FOR EVERY OCCASION

Lynda Burgess
and
Julia Tidmarsh

hamlyn

CROSS STITCH GREETING CARDS

Lynda Burgess and Julia Tidmarsh

First published in 1997 by Hamlyn
an imprint of Octopus Publishing Group Ltd
2–4 Heron Quays, London, E14 4JP

First published in paperback in 1999

Distributed in the United States by Sterling Publishing Co., Inc.
387 Park Avenue South, New York, NY 10016–8810

Publishing Director LAURA BAMFORD

Executive Editor SIMON TUITE
Project Editor KATIE COWAN
Editor CAROLINE BINGHAM

Art Director KEITH MARTIN
Executive Art Editor MARK STEVENS
Art Editor LISA TAI

Special Photography by LAURA WICKENDEN
Photograph on page 104-5 by DEBI TRELOAR
Illustrations by LESLEY WAKERLY

Production JOSEPHINE ALLUM and DAWN MITCHELL

The publishers have made every effort to ensure that all instructions given in this book are accurate and safe, but they cannot accept liability for any resulting injury, damage or loss to either person or property whether direct or consequential and howsoever arising. The author and publishers will be grateful for any information which will assist them in keeping future editions up-to-date.

Cataloguing-In-Publication-Data
A CIP catalogue for this book is available from the British Library.

ISBN: 0600 59930 2

Printed and bound in China

Contents

Introduction

Cross stitch and greeting cards are a combination which work well. So often stitchers accumulate boxes of work with lovingly stitched pictures, neatly stored and not touched for years. It's the stitching that's important and once it's in a stitcher's head to sew, nothing will stop them from doing so. However, if they're stitching for a purpose – for a celebration or a special occasion – the time spent sewing is so much more enjoyable, and a hand-stitched greeting card is always given from the heart. Much as they enjoy the stitching alone, a finished design, beautifully mounted and delivered to someone special, is one of the most satisfying moments for any cross stitcher.

Once mastered, cross stitch is an effective medium for creating superb pictures. It is often compared to painting by numbers, something I'm sure we've all turned our hand to at some time or other, usually with pretty dismal results. But only a stitcher can turn a colour chart into a work of art on canvas. Forget about the paintbrush –

with cross stitch everyone can become an artist, interpreting colours and symbols in their own way, and making every picture a personal triumph.

In **Cross Stitch Greeting Cards** you can choose from more than 50 original designs, all specially picked to celebrate the touching times of life. Some of Britain's best cross stitch designers have contributed to this collection. It spans from birth to retirement, covering all the precious moments in-between. And, if you're feeling inspired, turn to the motif library at the end of the book to add personal touches to your design.

I started sewing when I was eight. I can remember being handed some binca, thread and a piece of graph paper and being told to make it into a table mat. The teacher showed us the basic stitch and then left us to it. I have an extremely clear memory of designing and stitching a rooster into a corner of the fabric and then fraying the edges of the mat. It was great fun. I gave it to my mum as a present, she loved it, and the mat sat on top of the TV for the best part of the next ten years. As a child I had no inhibitions about stitching - I was shown how to do it and so I did. And as I've grown older I've approached every new craft with the same enthusiasm and lack of inhibition. It doesn't matter if you make mistakes, so long

as you have a go. You'll find you learn something from every mistake, until you feel confident enough to say you're an expert, and that's a lovely feeling. Talking to adults who have just started to cross stitch I've discovered that they've lost that childish lack of inhibition, and they often hinder themselves by thinking they're not able to learn something new. I'll tell you now, anyone can cross stitch and it's an addictive hobby that once started can easily turn into a way of life. You may start designing for books or magazines, start having your own kits made, or simply find all your spare time taken up with a needle in your hand.

Julia, my co-author, is a prime example of someone who started out with little confidence in her designs and stitching, yet as time moved on her confidence grew. She started experimenting and designing original work, rather than following other people's designs. With each new design she learnt something about how colours worked, which stitches to use where and how best to mount the finished work, up until now, when I would consider her to be one of the most talented designers I've worked with. Look out for her designs in this book, especially the dainty Easter Cross card and the subtly delicate Honeysuckle. This is the third book on which we have collaborated, and with every design I see she gets better.

In fact, each of the designers who've worked on this book have a distinctive style which you'll probably begin to recognize as you look through. And each has contributed something different from the other, which, hopefully, will mean that there's at least one design here for everyone, from quirky and comical to bold and colourful.

Use the designs as a starting point, and begin to make cards which you'll be proud to send. You'll find all instructions for making the cards on page 108, and instructions for mounting the cards on page 110. Then, as you gain confidence, use the motifs, borders, alphabets and numbers at the back of the book to add your own touch to your designs. For example, you could stitch the motorbike, give it a border and personalize it with a name, then instead of putting it in a card you could have it framed and give it as a present to be hung in a prime position in any home. Remember, you're creating heirlooms that'll be kept for ever. Your cross stitch pictures are your signature, something by which you'll be remembered, and the sentiments you send will be the things that trigger your recipient's memory. The more of yourself you put into a design, the more valued it will be by the recipient.

With greetings for all occasions, you should never find yourself short of ideas for every c o n c e i v a b l e celebration. So start stitching!

Births

If you've a friend or someone in the family who's expecting a baby,

mark the occasion with one of these original designs and let them know

how thrilled you are!

Moses Basket

Tucked away in the branches of a blossom tree, a new-born baby gets its first view of the world and everything that awaits him or her. It's an exciting event to capture in thread.

Measurements
The actual cross stitch design measures 10.5 x 6.8cm (4⅛ x 2¾in)

Materials
- 14.5 x 20cm (5¾ x 8in) of antique white 27-count evenweave fabric
- One skein of stranded cotton in each colour listed in the key
- Size 26 tapestry needle
- Green card with rectangular opening measuring 11 x 7.5cm (4¼ x 3in)

Note
Evenweave tends to fray more than Aida. Stop this happening by sealing the edge with nail varnish before you start stitching.

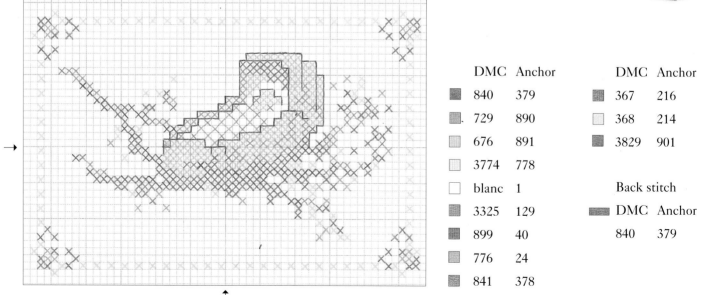

	DMC	Anchor
■	840	379
■	729	890
▨	676	891
▨	3774	778
□	blanc	1
▨	3325	129
■	899	40
▨	776	24
▨	841	378

	DMC	Anchor
▨	367	216
▨	368	214
■	3829	901

Back stitch

	DMC	Anchor
▬	840	379

Bear Repeat

Be there one, two, three or more babies at the same time, this cute teddy bear design can be adapted to suit.

Measurements

The actual cross stitch design measures
11.4 x 5.8cm (4½ x 2¼in)

Materials

- 13 x 15cm (5⅛ x 5⅞in) of white 18-count Aida fabric
- One skein of stranded cotton in each colour listed in the key
- Size 26 tapestry needle
- Pale green card with rectangular opening measuring 11.4 x 7cm (4½ x 2¾in)

Note

Choose the appropriate number and combination of girl or boy bears to suit the set of twins or triplets you are stitching for.

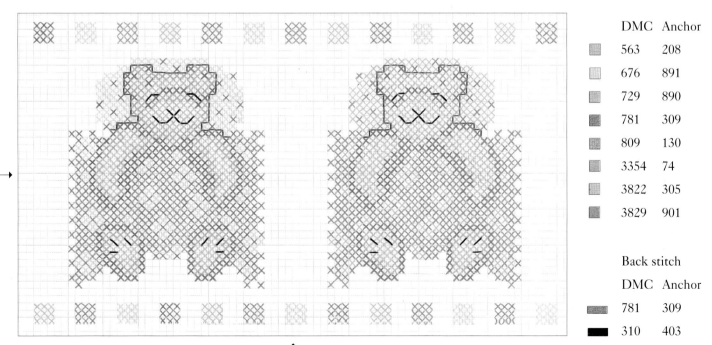

	DMC	Anchor
	563	208
	676	891
	729	890
	781	309
	809	130
	3354	74
	3822	305
	3829	901

Back stitch

	DMC	Anchor
	781	309
	310	403

Animal Sampler

If counting sheep appeals to you, why not try counting pigs, chickens and ducks, too?
This card would look fabulous framed and hung in a nursery.

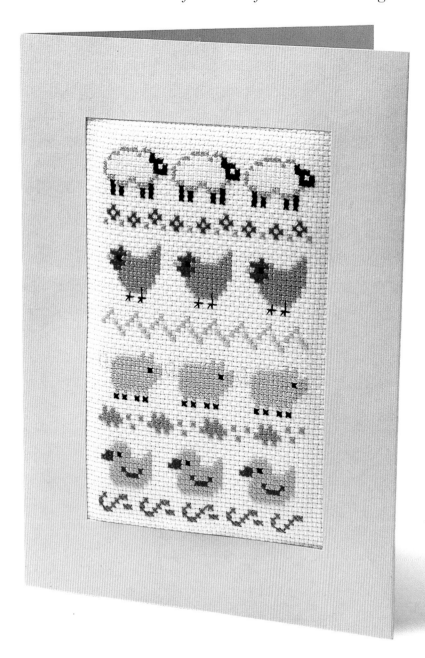

Measurements

The actual cross stitch design measures
8.3 x 13.3cm (3¼ x 5¼in)

Materials

- 14.5 x 20cm (5¾ x 8in) of white 14-count Aida fabric
- One skein of stranded cotton in each colour listed in the key
- Size 26 tapestry needle
- Pink card with rectangular opening measuring 9.5 x 14.5cm (3¾ x 5¾in)

Note

Individual animal motifs taken from this chart could be used to make gift tags or small items such as fridge magnets or keyrings.

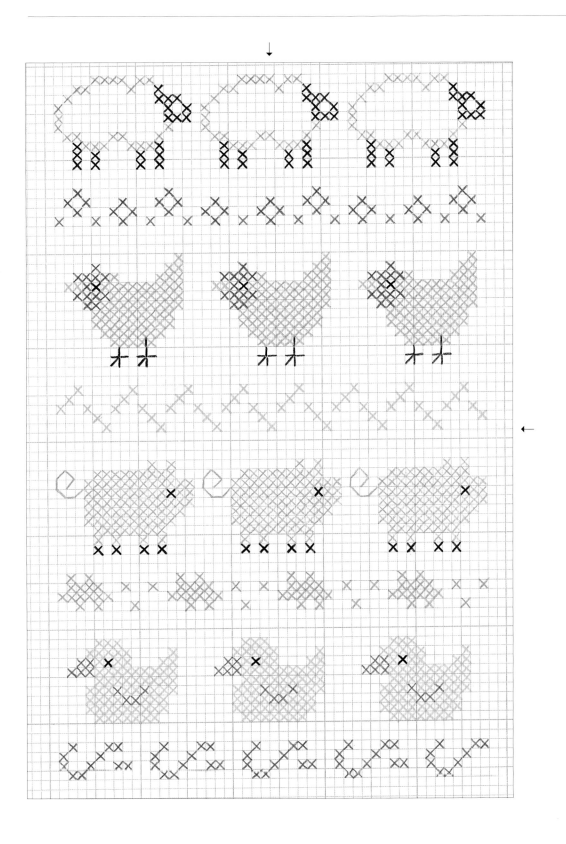

DMC Anchor
- 310 403
- 318 399
- 322 978
- 347 13
- 436 363
- 725 306
- 911 230
- 3689 49
- blanc 1

Back stitch
DMC Anchor
- 310 403
- 3689 49

Stork and Baby

Why not make this whimsical card for the proud parents-to-be to mark the imminent arrival of their new-born baby? Add a matching tag to decorate a gift.

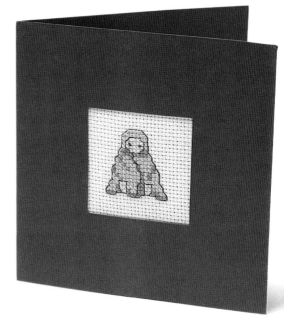

Measurements

Card: The actual cross stitch design measures 6.5 x 4.6cm (2⅝ x 1¾in)

Tag: The actual cross stitch design measures 2.5 x 2.6cm (1 x 1in)

Materials

- 13cm (5in) square of white 18-count Aida fabric for card
- 7.6cm (3in) square of white 18-count Aida fabric for tag
- One skein of stranded cotton in each colour listed in the keys
- Size 26 tapestry needle
- Pale blue (or pink) card with rectangular opening measuring 7.6 x 5.7 cm (3 x 2¼in)
- Blue (or pink) gift tag with square opening measuring 4 x 4cm (1½ x 1½in)

Note

If you want to personalize this design, you could make the baby's wrap a different colour and change all the blue to green, pink or yellow.

Card

DMC	Anchor
301	349
3072	397
972	298
597	168
3761	928
738	367
blanc	2

Back stitch

DMC	Anchor
3799	236

French knots

DMC	Anchor
3799	236

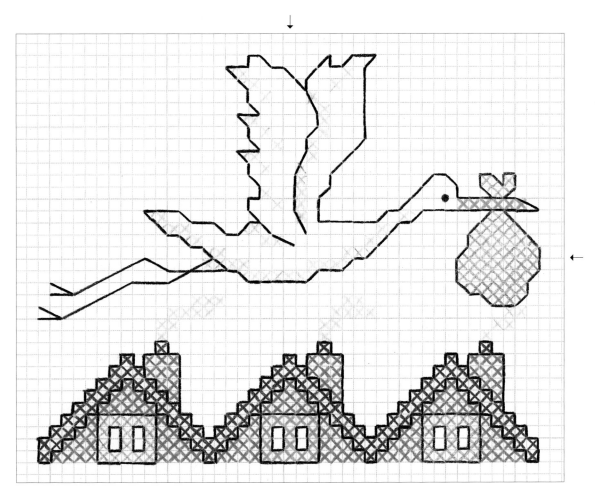

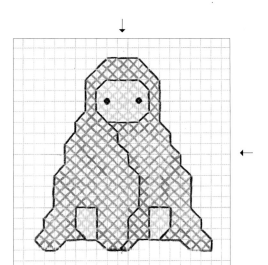

Tag for a boy

DMC	Anchor
819	271
597	168
3761	928

Back stitch

DMC	Anchor
3799	236

French knots

DMC	Anchor
3799	236

Tag for a girl

DMC	Anchor
819	271
962	75

Back stitch

DMC	Anchor
3799	236

French knots

DMC	Anchor
3799	236

Toy Sampler

Why not make a card that's as much a gift as it is a greeting? You could frame this nursery design and it would provide a welcome and permanent reminder of childhood.

Measurements

The actual cross stitch design measures 12.2 x 8.5cm (4⅞ x 3⅜in)

Materials

- 14.5 x 20cm (5¾ x 8in) of white 14-count Aida fabric
- One skein of stranded cotton in each colour listed in the key

- Size 26 tapestry needle
- Red card with rectangular opening measuring 15 x 10cm (6 x 4in)

Note

Use the numbers and alphabets from the back of the book to personalize this card, with a name and date of birth.

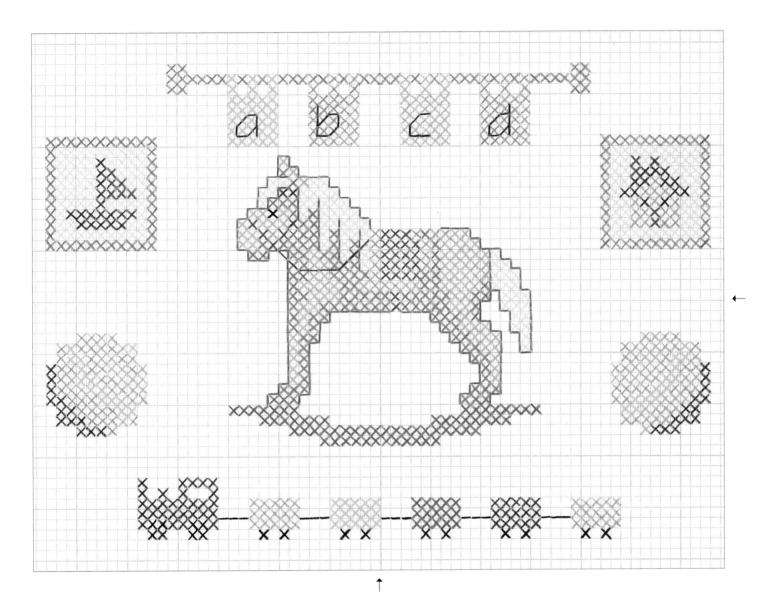

	DMC	Anchor		DMC	Anchor	Back stitch			
■	310	403	▨	563	208	DMC	Anchor		
▨	322	978	▨	677	300	▨	347	13	alphabet
▨	347	13	▨	726	295	▨	322	978	horse's reins
▨	435	901	▨	809	130	▨	435	901	horse's body and mane
▨	436	363	▨	3689	49	■	310	403	train
▨	562	210							

BIRTHDAYS

There's nothing more special than a thoughtfully stitched greeting for a friend or loved one. A hand-made card is also a gift that'll be kept and treasured for ever.

Little Girl's 1st Birthday

Mark the occasion of this first, special birthday with a party, a present and a hand-stitched card to harness and savour the memory.

Measurements

The actual cross stitch design measures 7.3 x 6.8cm (2⅞ x 2¾in)

Materials

- 13cm (5in) square of white 18-count Aida fabric
- One skein of stranded cotton in each colour listed in the key
- Size 26 tapestry needle
- Pink card with square opening measuring 8.8 x 8.8cm (3½ x 3½in)

	DMC	Anchor
	666	46
	601	77
	604	55
	353	6
	996	433
	975	370
	976	309
	310	403
	blanc	1

Back stitch

	DMC	Anchor
	310	403

French knots

	DMC	Anchor
••	310	403

Little Boy's 1st Birthday

Remember the first birthday, the first cake and the first candle to be blown out? Capture a magic moment which can never be revisited.

Measurements
The actual cross stitch design measures 6.5 x 6.8cm (2⅝ x 2¾in)

Materials
- 13cm (5in) square of white 18-count Aida fabric
- One skein of stranded cotton in each colour listed in the key
- Size 26 tapestry needle
- Blue card with square opening measuring 8.8 x 8.8cm (3½ x 3½in)

Note
Use the large numbers from the back of this book to make this card suitable for any age of child.

	DMC	Anchor
	797	132
	996	433
	823	150
	353	6
	702	226
	666	46
	743	305
	975	370
	310	403

Back stitch

	DMC	Anchor
	310	403

French knots

	DMC	Anchor
• •	310	403

Girl's 18th Birthday

A pretty, feminine arrangement of ribbons, flowers and the key to the door makes a memorable card for that special 18th birthday.

Measurements

The actual cross stitch design measures 7.2 x 5cm (2⅞ x 2in)

Materials

- 13cm (5in) square of white 14-count Aida fabric
- One skein of stranded cotton in each colour listed in the key
- Size 26 tapestry needle
- Lilac card with rectangular opening measuring 8 x 5.7cm (3⅛ x 2¼in)

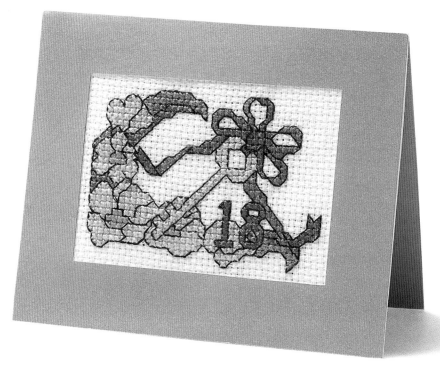

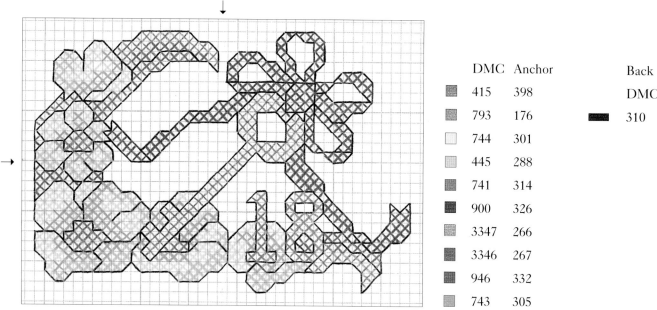

	DMC	Anchor
	415	398
	793	176
	744	301
	445	288
	741	314
	900	326
	3347	266
	3346	267
	946	332
	743	305

Back stitch

	DMC	Anchor
	310	403

Girl's 18th or 21st

The wild rose is a beautiful flower and an extremely popular subject for cross stitch. It makes a lovely card for an 18th or 21st birthday.

Measurements
The actual cross stitch design measures 4.5 x 6.8cm (1¾ x 2¾in)

Materials
- 13cm (5in) square of white 14-count Aida fabric
- One skein of stranded cotton in each colour listed in the key
- Size 26 tapestry needle
- Red card with oval opening measuring 5 x 7.5cm (2 x 3in)

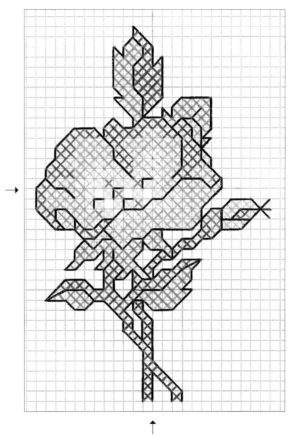

	DMC	Anchor		DMC	Anchor
	700	228		712	926
	701	227		445	288
	699	229		762	234
	913	204			
	335	41		Back stitch	
	3326	36		DMC	Anchor
	818	48		310	403
	819	271			

Boy's 18th or 21st

At an age to play, to break the ties and zoom off into the fast lane, this design makes an ideal card. Choose it to mark an eighteenth or twenty-first birthday celebration.

Measurements
The actual cross stitch design measures 13.6 x 8cm (5⅜ x 3⅛in)

Materials
• 14.5 x 20cm (5¾ x 8in) of cream 28-count evenweave fabric
• One skein of stranded cotton in each colour listed in the key
• Size 26 tapestry needle

• Red card with rectangular opening measuring 14.5 x 9.5cm (5¾ x 3¾in)

Note
Omit the number and key from this card to make an ideal greeting for any motorbike enthusiast. A line shows the edge of white cross stitch behind the seat. Do not work as back stitch.

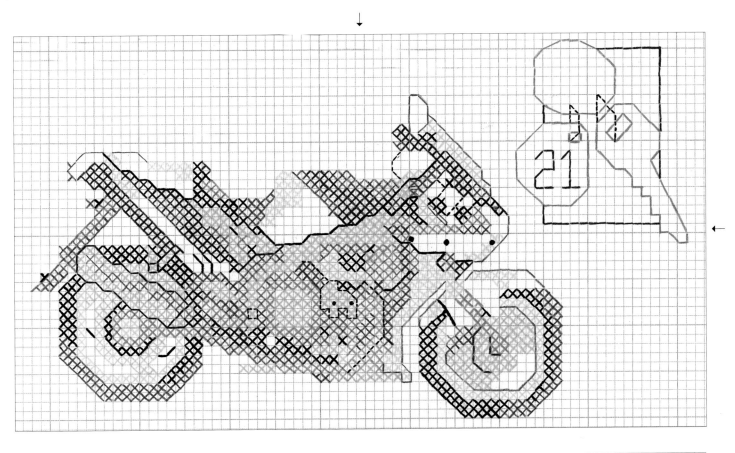

	DMC	Anchor		DMC	Anchor	Back stitch			
■	310	403		928	847	1 strand			
	350	11		3072	274	DMC	Anchor		
	413	401	□	blanc	1	------	310	403	key chain, engine
	422	943					646	8581	front mudguard, fairing
	543	933		French knots					
	646	8581		DMC	Anchor	Back stitch			
	648	900	• • •	310	403	2 strands			
	666	46				DMC	Anchor		
	712	926					310	403	under seat and petrol tank
	721	324					648	900	key and key fob
	840	379					666	46	numerals and box around key
	812	376					840	379	main exhaust pipes
	844	273					blanc	1	handlebars

Boy's 18th or 21st

Think of a favourite pastime and create a card which is unique to the person who'll receive it. In this case, the football fan will be happy.

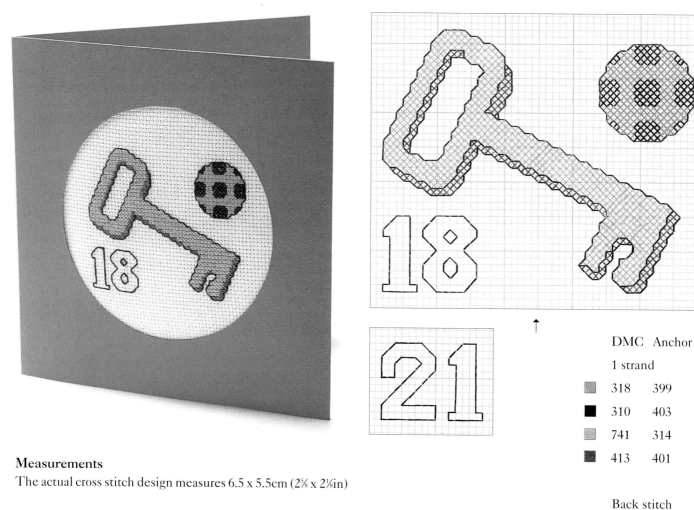

DMC	Anchor
1 strand	
318	399
310	403
741	314
413	401

Back stitch	
DMC	Anchor
310	403

Measurements

The actual cross stitch design measures 6.5 x 5.5cm (2⅝ x 2⅛in)

Materials

- 13cm (5in) square of white 18-count Aida fabric
- One skein of stranded cotton in each colour listed in the key
- Size 26 tapestry needle
- Blue card with 8.3cm (3¼in) diameter circular opening

Man's 70th/80th/90th Birthday

At the time of life when all one wants to do is relax and reminisce, this card will trigger memories of all the recipient's favourite hobbies.

Measurements

The actual cross stitch design measures 7.2 x 6.2cm (2⅞ x 2½in)

Materials

- 13cm (5in) square of white 18-count Aida fabric
- One skein of stranded cotton in each colour listed in the key
- Size 26 tapestry needle
- Bright green card with square opening measuring 8 x 8cm (3⅛ x 3⅛in)

Note

If, after stitching, you find your work has become a little dirty, wash it in lukewarm water in a mild solution of washing-up liquid. Leave it to soak, then rinse. Do not wring it out, just dry on a flat surface.

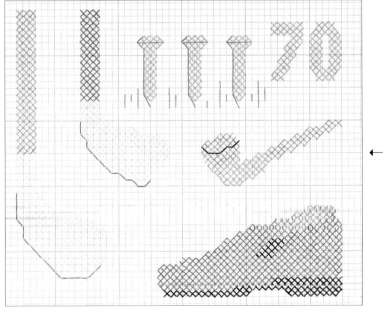

DMC	Anchor		Back stitch		
1 strand			DMC	Anchor	
954	225		310	403	pipe
781	309		924	849	golf tees and
301	349				club heads
738	361		954	225	grass
3072	847				
927	849				
310	403				

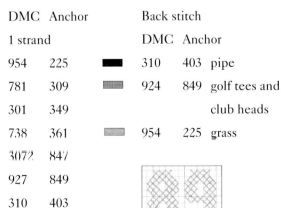

Woman's 70th/80th/90th Birthday

The impact of dainty violets pouring out from the top of this flower-filled basket make this a spectacular card. Choose it as a card to send on a friend or relative's retirement.

Measurements
The actual cross stitch design measures 10.8 x 8.5cm (4¼ x 3⅜in)

Materials
- 20 x 14.5cm (8 x 5¾in) of white 28-count evenweave fabric
- One skein of stranded cotton in each colour listed in the key

- Size 26 tapestry needle
- Purple card with rectangular opening measuring 14.5 x 9.5cm (5¾ x 3¾in)

Note
Always stitch over two threads when working on evenweave, to give the same final measurements as over one block of Aida.

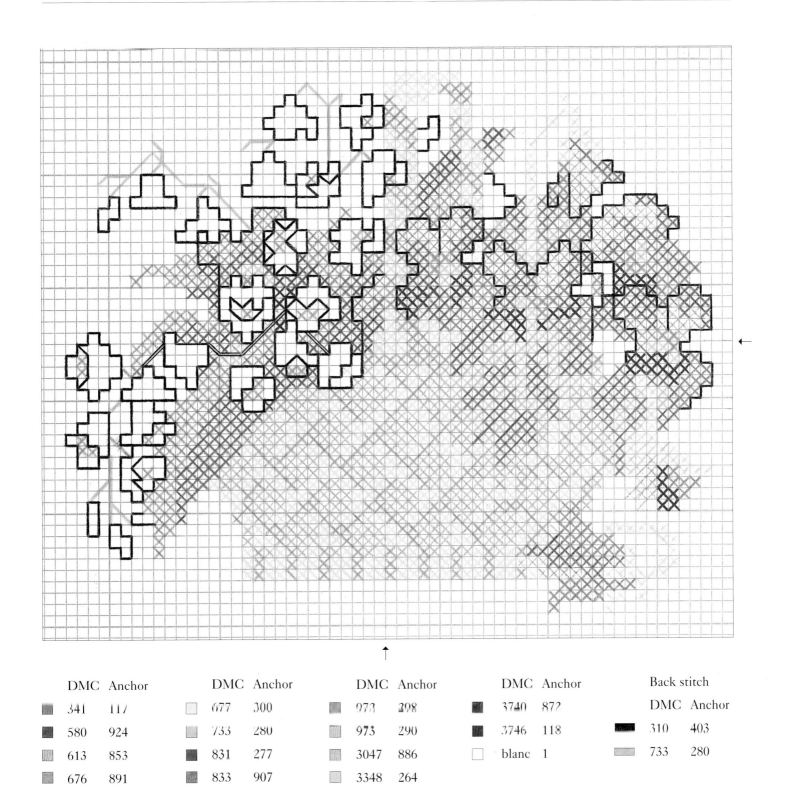

DMC	Anchor		DMC	Anchor		DMC	Anchor		DMC	Anchor		Back stitch
												DMC	Anchor
341	117		677	300		973	298		3740	872		310	403
580	924		733	280		973	290		3746	118		733	280
613	853		831	277		3047	886		blanc	1			
676	891		833	907		3348	264						

ENGAGEMENTS AND WEDDINGS

Who's getting married in the morning? Whoever it is, you won't be the one to miss the celebration. Join in the merriment and sew!

Engagement Congratulations

It could be the happiest day of your life, and it's certainly one which will be remembered for ever. Take the tipple and stitch this design to commemorate the day.

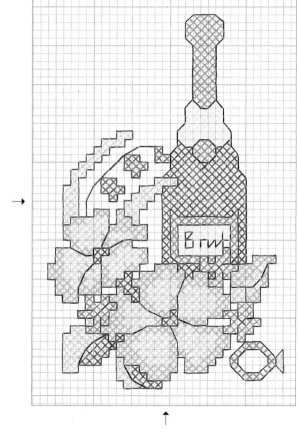

Measurements

The actual cross stitch
design measures 4.5 x 6.8cm (1¾ x 2¾in)

Materials

- 13cm (5in) square of white 18-count Aida fabric
- One skein of stranded cotton in each colour listed in the key
- Size 26 tapestry needle
- Yellow card with rectangular opening measuring 5.7 x 7.5cm (2¼ x 3in)

Note

You could make this card equally suitable for a wedding by omitting to
stitch the diamond on the ring.

	DMC	Anchor		DMC	Anchor
	973	290		502	877
	783	306		746	386
	445	288			
	210	108		Back stitch	
	776	24		DMC	Anchor
	368	214		801	358

Wedding Congratulations

Tying the knot is a big step and probably one of the biggest things to change your life. Let the happy couple know how pleased you are for them on their big day.

Measurements

The actual cross stitch design measures 4.8 x 6.5cm (1⅞ x 2⅝in)

Materials

• 13cm (5in) square of white 18-count Aida fabric
• One skein of stranded cotton in each colour listed in the key
• Size 26 tapestry needle
• White card with rectangular opening measuring 5.7 x 7.5cm (2¼ x 3in)

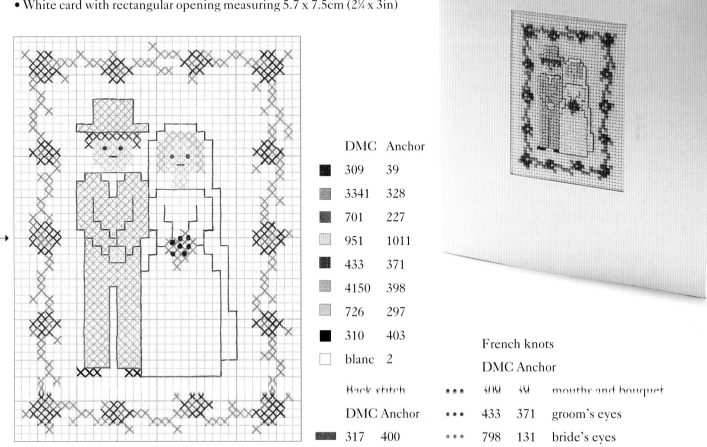

DMC	Anchor
309	39
3341	328
701	227
951	1011
433	371
4150	398
726	297
310	403
blanc	2

Back stitch

DMC	Anchor
317	400

French knots

DMC	Anchor	
309	39	mouths and bouquet
433	371	groom's eyes
798	131	bride's eyes

Wedding Congratulations and Place Card

This elegant wedding greeting makes a perfect gift for the happy couple and is guaranteed to be treasured. Add place cards for the top table, or even every guest if you're very ambitious.

Measurements

Card: The actual cross stitch design measures 8 x 13.2cm (3⅛ x 5¼in)

Place card: The actual cross stitch design measures 5.3 x 3.8cm (2⅛ x 1½in)

Materials

- 14.5 x 20cm (5¾ x 8in) of white 14-count Aida fabric for card
- 7.5 x 10cm (3 x 4in) of white 18-count Aida fabric for place card
- One skein of stranded cotton in each colour listed in the key
- Size 26 tapestry needle
- Salmon pink card with rectangular opening measuring 9 x 14cm (3½ x 5½in)
- Salmon pink gift tag with rectangular opening measuring 6.2 x 4.6cm (2½ x 1¾in)

Note

To make the place card, choose a corner of the main design and stitch it on to a small piece of fabric which can then be mounted into the tag. Cross stitch the place card with one strand of thread.

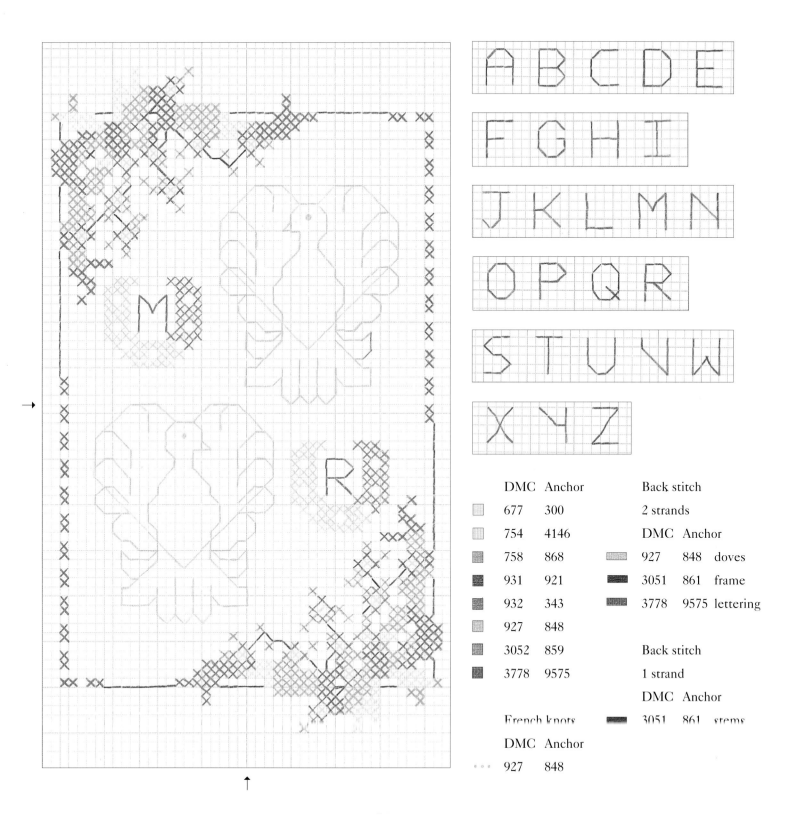

A B C D E

F G H I

J K L M N

O P Q R

S T U V W

X Y Z

DMC	Anchor
677	300
754	4146
758	868
931	921
932	343
927	848
3052	859
3778	9575

French knots

DMC	Anchor
927	848

Back stitch
2 strands

DMC	Anchor	
927	848	doves
3051	861	frame
3778	9575	lettering

Back stitch
1 strand

DMC	Anchor	
3051	861	stems

Wedding Sampler

These peaceful doves and gold rings intertwined as a symbol of nascent love make a touching sentiment for a perfect match.

Measurements
The actual cross stitch design measures
9 x 14.3cm (3½ x 5⅝in)

Materials
• 14.5 x 20cm (5¾ x 8in) of antique white
   27-count evenweave fabric
• One skein of stranded cotton in each colour
   listed in the key
• Size 26 tapestry needle
• White card with rectangular opening
   measuring 10.5 x 15.7cm (4⅛ x 6⅛in)

Note
Why not add the initials of the bride and groom to this card for a truly personal gift? You'll find a selection of letters beginning on page 98.

DMC   Anchor

☐ blanc   1

■ 3350   78

▨ 3687   68

▨ 776   25

▨ 762   234

▨ 1 strand DMC 725
(Anchor 305) with
1 strand gold thread

▨ 1 strand DMC 762
(Anchor 234) with
1 strand silver thread

Back stitch
DMC   Anchor

▬ 3350   78   ribbon

▬ 762   234   doves' outlines

▬ 317   400   wings, bells, rings

French knots
DMC Anchor

••• 317   400

Silver Anniversary

Let the bells ring out to 25 years of wedded bliss! Now that's something which should be celebrated. Stitch these sparkling silver bells for a special congratulatory greeting.

Measurements

The actual cross stitch design measures 7.5 x 12.4cm (3 x 4⅞in)

Materials

- 14.5 x 20cm (5¾ x 8in) of antique white 27-count evenweave fabric
- One skein of stranded cotton in each colour listed in the key
- Size 26 tapestry needle
- Lavender card with oval opening measuring 9.5 x 14.5cm (3¾ x 5¾in)

Note

If you'd like to personalize this card, use one of the alphabets from the back of the book. Use transparent grid paper to trace the letters from the chart and then transfer them on to the design.

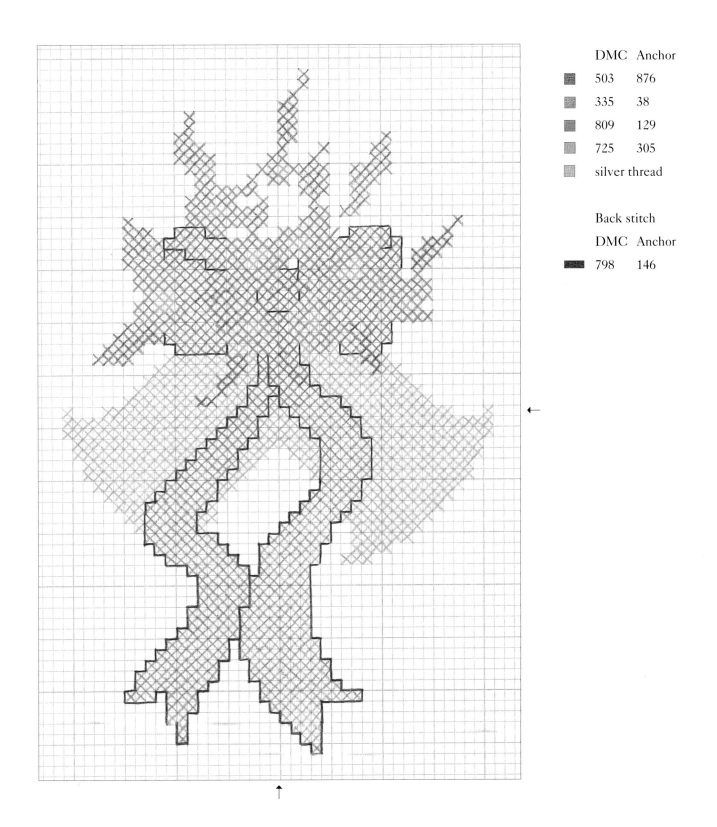

DMC	Anchor
503	876
335	38
809	129
725	305
silver thread	

Back stitch

DMC	Anchor
798	146

GOOD LUCK

There's a great sense of achievement every time you accomplish something that could change your life. Here are a selection of cards to commemorate those moments, and one or two that simply wish 'good luck!'.

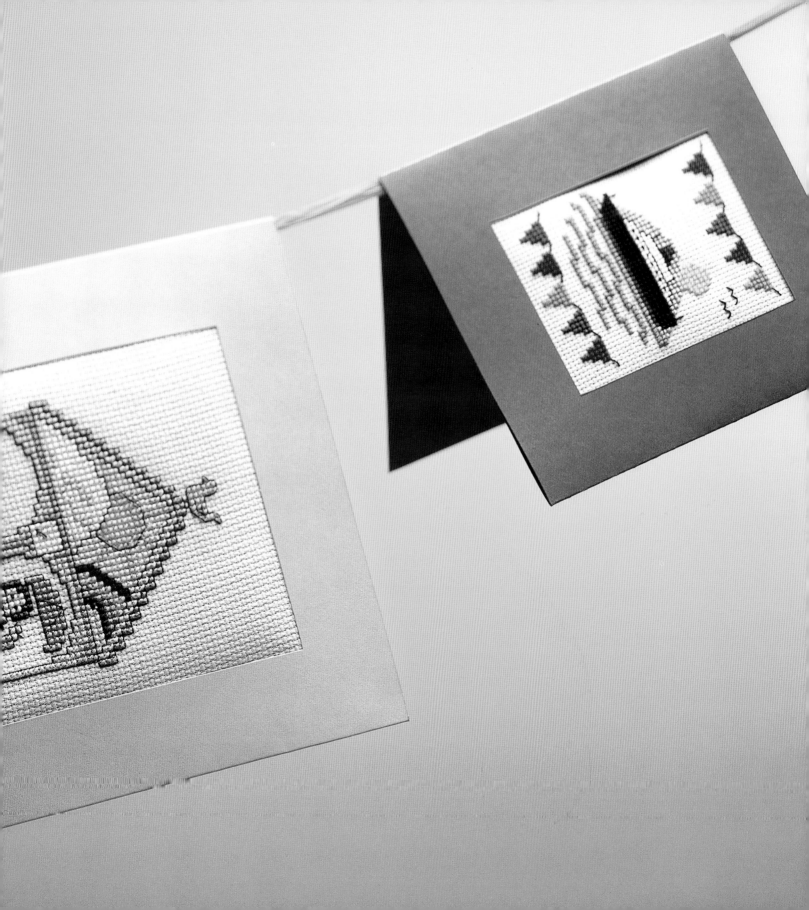

Good Luck

We all deserve a little good luck. Let someone know you wish them well and send them this optimistic and quick to stitch greeting.

Measurements

The actual cross stitch design measures 5 x 7.2cm (2 x 2⅞in)

Materials

- 13 x 15cm (5 x 6in) of white 18-count Aida fabric
- One skein of stranded cotton in each colour listed in the key
- Size 26 tapestry needle
- Dark blue card with oval opening measuring 6.8 x 10cm (2¾ x 4in)

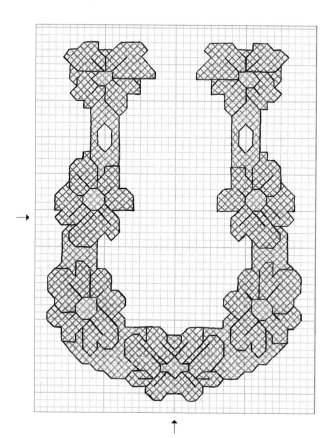

	DMC	Anchor
	834	874
	793	122
	524	858

Back stitch

	DMC	Anchor
▬	310	403

New Job

Changing your job is a stressful experience, yet we all know how a change can be as good as a rest. Mark the changes with this congratulatory card.

Measurements

The actual cross stitch design measures 7.3 x 5cm (2⅞ x 2in)

Materials

- 13cm (5in) square of white 18-count Aida fabric
- One skein of stranded cotton in each colour listed in the key
- Size 26 tapestry needle
- Bright green card with rectangular opening measuring 7.6 x 5.7cm (3 x 2¼in)

Note

This card would be equally appropriate to celebrate a promotion at work.

	DMC	Anchor		DMC	Anchor
▨	414	235	▨	958	187
▨	453	231	▨	704	238
▨	3078	292			
▨	975	370		**Back stitch**	
▨	3828	373		DMC	Anchor
▨	444	291	▬	740	316	dress
▨	740	316	▬	975	370	legs, mouth, hands
▨	353	6	▬	958	187	flower stems
▨	666	46	▬	414	235	wall chart
■	310	403			
☐	blanc	1		**French knots**	
▨	519	167		DMC	Anchor
			•••	975	370

New Home

Moving house is one of the biggest, most expensive and considered decisions ever. It's certainly not an event that should go unnoticed.

Measurements
The actual cross stitch design measures
7.6 x 12.4cm (3⅛ x 4¾n)

Materials
- 14.5 x 20cm (5¾ x 8in) of white 14-count Aida fabric
- One skein of stranded cotton in each colour listed in the key
- Size 26 tapestry needle
- Light green card with rectangular opening measuring 9.5 x 14.5cm (3¾ x 5¾in)

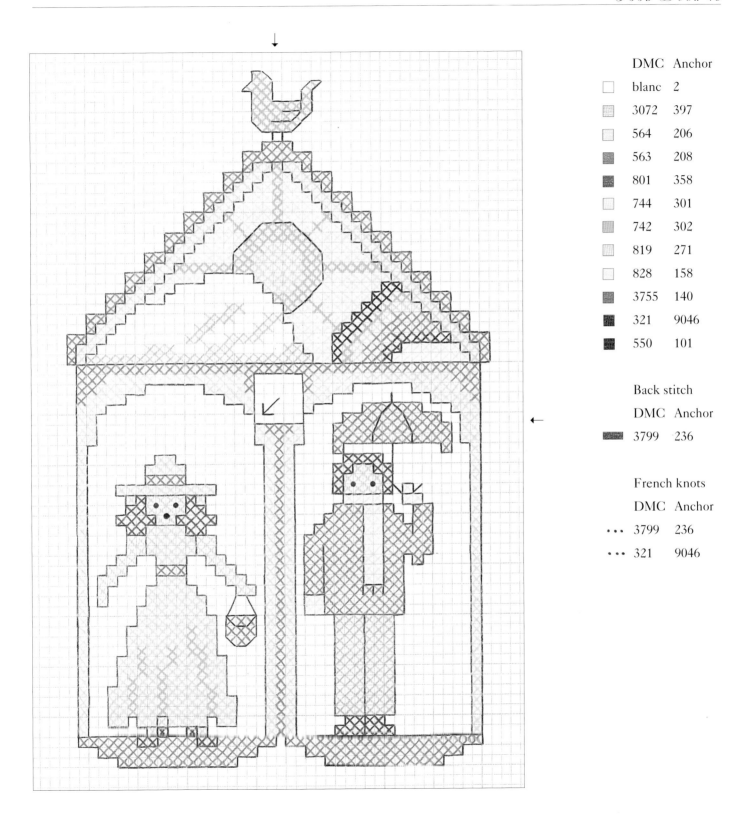

DMC Anchor

blanc 2
3072 397
564 206
563 208
801 358
744 301
742 302
819 271
828 158
3755 140
321 9046
550 101

Back stitch
DMC Anchor
3799 236

French knots
DMC Anchor
••• 3799 236
••• 321 9046

Exams

Hats off to the person with the results. A big celebration is in order, whether the recipient has sat a degree, passed school exams or achieved a professional set.

Measurements

The actual cross stitch design measures 5 x 6.5cm (2 x 2⅜in)

Materials

- 13cm (5in) square of white 18-count Aida fabric
- One skein of stranded cotton in each colour listed in the key
- Size 26 tapestry needle
- Dark green card with rectangular opening measuring 5.7 x 7.5cm (2¼ x 3in)

To make a tassel

1 Cut two pieces of thin card approximately 3cm (1⅛in) wide and place together.

2 Wind a length of stranded cotton (all six strands) several times around both cards.

3 Pass a needle containing one strand of cotton between the cards and tie the tassel together at one end. Leave the ends of this thread long.

4 Cut through the tassel at the other end and then remove the cards. Keeping the threads folded in half, wind a single strand around the top of the tassel several times. Pass the end of this strand through the wound thread to cast off.

5 Use the thread from stage 3 to stitch the tassel onto the card as indicated on the chart.

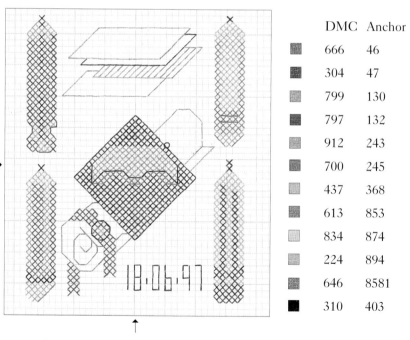

	DMC	Anchor
	666	46
	304	47
	799	130
	797	132
	912	243
	700	245
	437	368
	613	853
	834	874
	224	894
	646	8581
	310	403

o   position for tassel

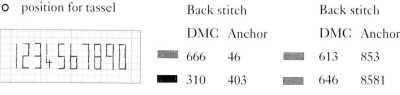

Back stitch			Back stitch		
	DMC	Anchor		DMC	Anchor
	666	46		613	853
	310	403		646	8581

Travel or Moving Abroad

If a friend moves abroad or takes an extended trek into the wide blue yonder, this card will fit the occasion perfectly.

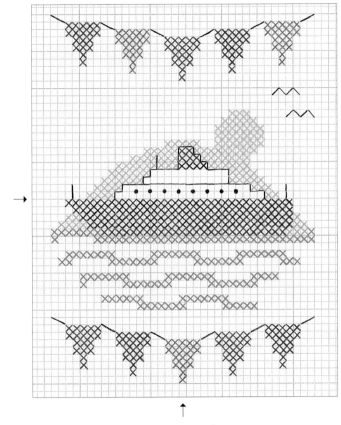

Measurements

The actual cross stitch design measures 5.2 x 7.6cm (2¹⁄₁₆ x 3in)

Materials

- 13cm (5in) square of white 18-count Aida fabric
- One skein of stranded cotton in each colour listed in the key
- Size 26 tapestry needle
- Blue card with rectangular opening measuring 5.7 x 8.3cm (2¼ x 3¼in)

	DMC	Anchor		DMC	Anchor	French knots	
■	310	403	▧	519	167		DMC	Anchor
▧	726	295	▦	958	187	•••	310	403
▦	666	46						
▦	740	316			Back stitch		
☐	blanc	1			DMC	Anchor	
▦	797	132	▬	310	403		

Driving Test

You've cause for celebration if you've just passed your driving test. This is definitely a card for a careful driver. Who do you know who deserves one?

Measurements
The actual cross stitch design measures 13.2 x 8cm (5¼ x 3⅛in)

Materials
• 14.5 x 20cm (5¾ x 8in) of white 14-count Aida fabric

• One skein of stranded cotton in each colour listed in the key
• Size 26 tapestry needle
• Dark green card with retangular opening measuring 14.5 x 9.5cm (5¾ x 3¾in)

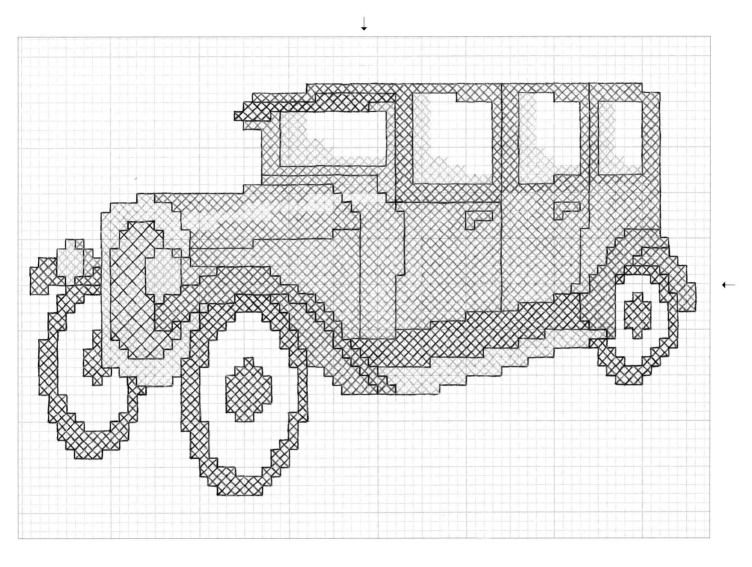

DMC	Anchor		DMC	Anchor		Back stitch	
3032	832		318	399		**DMC**	**Anchor**
783	306		524	858		310	403
310	403		3362	263			
blanc	2		3363	262			
640	393		522	860			

Visit to Hospital

The rabbit's in a sorry state with his bandaged ear and paw, but he's sure to cheer up anybody who's not feeling one hundred per cent.

Measurements

The actual cross stitch design measures 5.5 x 8cm (2⅛ x 3⅛in)

Materials

- 13 x 15cm (5 x 6in) of white 18-count Aida fabric
- One skein of stranded cotton in each colour listed in the key
- Size 26 tapestry needle
- Turquoise card with rectangular opening measuring 6.2 x 8.5cm (2½ x 3⅜in)

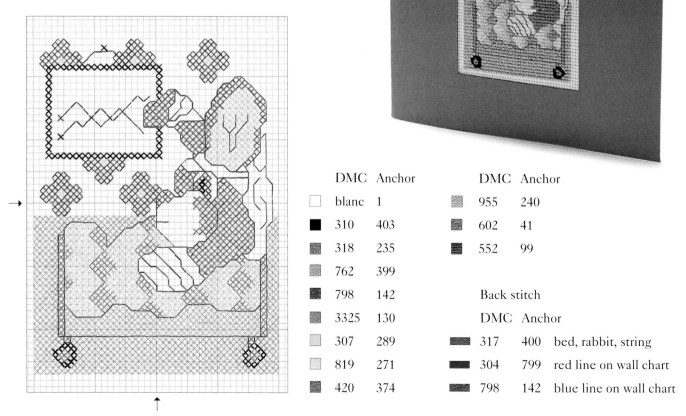

	DMC	Anchor			DMC	Anchor	
	blanc	1			955	240	
	310	403			602	41	
	318	235			552	99	
	762	399					
	798	142			**Back stitch**		
	3325	130			DMC	Anchor	
	307	289			317	400	bed, rabbit, string
	819	271			304	799	red line on wall chart
	420	374			798	142	blue line on wall chart

Get Well Soon

They say flowers are always appreciated and cheering. Why not give flowers to someone you know who's a little under the weather?

Measurements

The actual cross stitch design measures 4.7 x 6.5cm
(1⅞ x 2⅝in)

Materials

- 13cm (5in) square of white 18-count Aida fabric
- One skein of stranded cotton in each colour listed in the key
- Size 26 tapestry needle
- Red card with rectangular opening measuring 7 x 9cm (2¾ x 3½in)

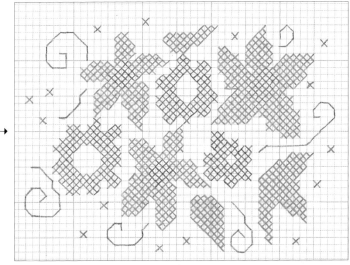

DMC	Anchor		Back stitch	
1 strand			DMC	Anchor
3778	9575		3042	870
3726	970			
977	313			
3042	870			

SPECIAL OCCASIONS

Mark key days in the year with a stitched greeting card to help your family and friends remember those days over the years to come.

Happy New Year

Let the New Year in with a celebration tipple and look forward to the promising times ahead.

Measurements

The actual cross stitch design measures 5 x 7.3cm (2 x 2⅞in)

Materials

- 13cm (5in) square of white 18-count Aida fabric
- One skein of stranded cotton in each colour listed in the key
- Size 26 tapestry needle
- Blue card with rectangular opening measuring 6 x 8cm (2⅜ x 3⅛in)

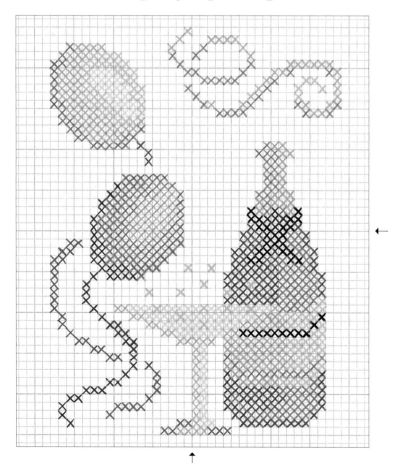

	DMC	Anchor		DMC	Anchor
	209	109		677	300
	310	403		783	307
	327	100		815	22
	553	98		3765	169
	554	97		3812	189
	646	8581		3818	246
	648	900		3820	874
	676	891			

New Year Chimney Sweep

People used to believe a chimney sweep brought luck for the New Year. Welcome a sweep into a friend's home with this cheerful card.

Measurements

The actual cross stitch design measures 5 x 7.5cm (2 x 3in)

Materials

- 13 x 15cm (5 x 6in) of white 18-count Aida fabric
- One skein of stranded cotton in each colour listed in the key
- Size 26 tapestry needle
- Bright red card with rectangular opening measuring 7.5 x 10cm (3 x 4in)

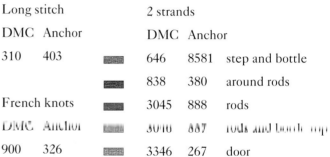

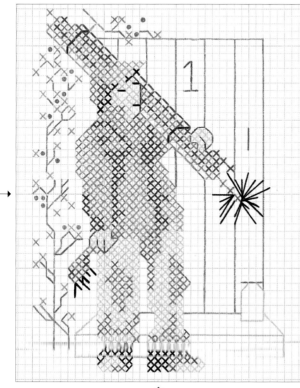

	DMC	Anchor
■	310	403
	646	8581
	838	380
	840	379
	841	378
	844	273
	900	326
	951	880
	3045	888
	3046	887
	3346	267
□	3770	276

Long stitch

	DMC	Anchor
—	310	403

French knots

	DMC	Anchor
••••	900	326

Back stitch

1 strand

	DMC	Anchor	
■	310	403	face
	840	379	branches
	844	273	around face, hands and door knob

Back stitch

2 strands

	DMC	Anchor	
	646	8581	step and bottle
	838	380	around rods
	3045	888	rods
	3046	887	rods and bench top
	3346	267	door

Valentine's Day

Keep him guessing with this Victorian-inspired, hand-stitched Valentine Day's card.

Measurements

The actual cross stitch design measures 7.7 x 7.8cm (3¹⁄₁₆ x 3¹⁄₁₆in)

Materials

- 13cm (5in) square of antique white 27-count evenweave fabric
- One skein of stranded cotton in each colour listed in the key
- Size 26 tapestry needle
- Pink card with square opening measuring 8.6 x 8.6cm (3⅜ x 3⅜in)

DMC	Anchor		Back stitch	
			DMC	Anchor
963	73			
677	885		3350	65
962	75		3051	861
523	859			

Note

Before you send this card, why not add a couple of drops of scent to add a further air of mystery? No one will ever know who sent it!

Easter Chick

Choose this cute, newly-born chick to make an enchanting Easter card.

Measurements

The actual cross stitch design measures 7.1 x 6cm (2¾ x 2⅜in)

Materials

- 13cm (5in) square of white 18-count Aida fabric

- One skein of stranded cotton in each colour listed in the key
- Size 26 tapestry needle
- Yellow card with 8.3cm (3¼in) diameter circular opening

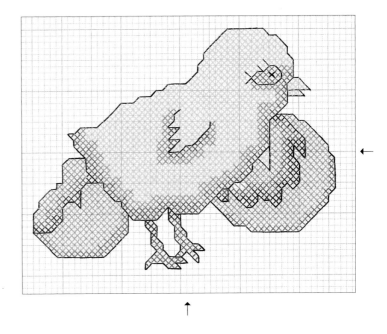

	DMC	Anchor		DMC	Anchor
▦	898	360	■	310	403
▦	435	369	▦	3325	976
▦	437	368			
▦	721	324		Back stitch	
▦	977	313		DMC	Anchor
▢	445	288	▬	310	403

Easter Cross

Remember the true meaning of Easter with this attractively dainty, seasonal greeting.

Measurements
The actual cross stitch design measures 4.3 x 6.5cm (1¾ x 2⅝in)

Materials
- 13cm (5in) square of white 18-count Aida fabric
- One skein of stranded cotton in each colour listed in the key
- Size 26 tapestry needle
- Yellow card with rectangular opening measuring 5.7 x 7.5cm (2¼ x 3in)

	DMC	Anchor		Back stitch	
	3072	397		DMC	Anchor
	445	288		801	358
	973	290			
	437	368			
	972	298			
	742	303			
	772	259			
	471	265			

Mother's Day

Let your mother know how much you care by making her this original card.

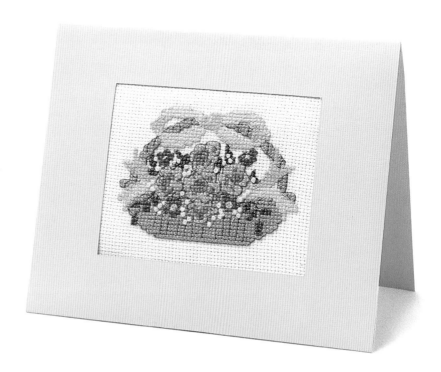

Measurements

The actual cross stitch design measures 5.5 x 8cm (2⅛ x 3⅛in)

Materials

- 13 x 15cm (5 x 6in) of white 18-count Aida fabric
- One skein of stranded cotton in each colour listed in the key
- Size 26 tapestry needle
- Yellow card with rectangular opening measuring 6.2 x 8.5cm (2½ x 3⅜in)

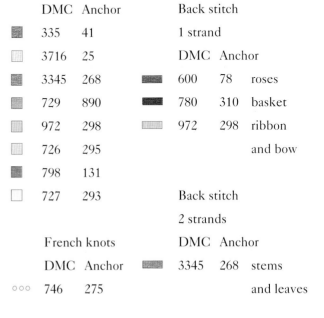

	DMC	Anchor
▨	335	41
▢	3716	25
▨	3345	268
▨	729	890
▨	972	298
▨	726	295
▨	798	131
▢	727	293

French knots

	DMC	Anchor
○○○	746	275

Back stitch
1 strand

	DMC	Anchor	
▬	600	78	roses
▬	780	310	basket
▬	972	298	ribbon and bow

Back stitch
2 strands

	DMC	Anchor	
▬	3345	268	stems and leaves

Father's Day

As the years pass by, picture this tranquil scene, epitomizing the luxury of having time on your hands to do with as you will.

Measurements

The actual cross stitch design measures 8 x 14.3cm (3⅛ x 5⅝in)

Materials

- 14.5 x 20cm (5¾ x 8in) of white 14-count Aida fabric
- One skein of stranded cotton in each colour listed in the key
- Size 26 tapestry needle
- Bright blue card with rectangular opening measuring 9 x 15cm (3½ x 6in)

Note

There are a lot of threads for this card. Keep them handy by making your own thread sorter out of the cardboard from tights or shirt packaging.

To make a thread sorter

1 Use a hole punch to make holes down the side of a piece of thin card. Make as many holes as there are threads used in the design.
2 Number each hole with the appropriate thread number.
3 Loop cut lengths of the threads through the appropriate hole.

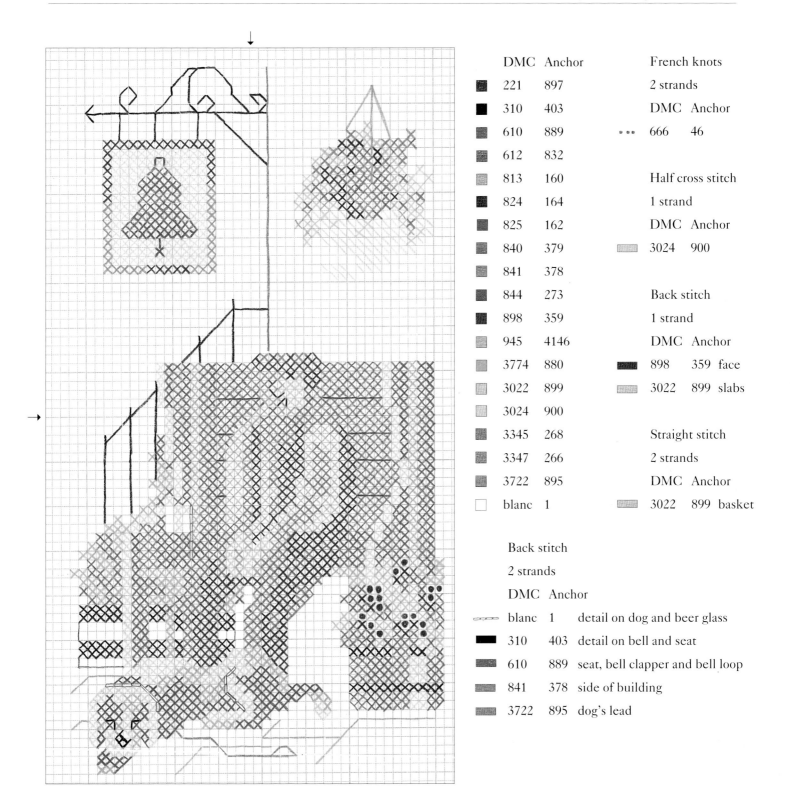

DMC	Anchor
221	897
310	403
610	889
612	832
813	160
824	164
825	162
840	379
841	378
844	273
898	359
945	4146
3774	880
3022	899
3024	900
3345	268
3347	266
3722	895
blanc	1

French knots

2 strands

DMC	Anchor
666	46

Half cross stitch

1 strand

DMC	Anchor
3024	900

Back stitch

1 strand

DMC	Anchor	
898	359	face
3022	899	slabs

Straight stitch

2 strands

DMC	Anchor	
3022	899	basket

Back stitch

2 strands

DMC	Anchor	
blanc	1	detail on dog and beer glass
310	403	detail on bell and seat
610	889	seat, bell clapper and bell loop
841	378	side of building
3722	895	dog's lead

CHRISTMAS

A Christmas cross stitch greeting can be brought out year after year as part of

the Yuletide decorations.

Santa

If you're looking for a challenging and substantial project, have a go at stitching Santa. He'd make a perfect card, or you could frame him instead!

Measurements
The actual cross stitch design measures
13 x 8.2cm (5 x 3¼in)

Materials
- 14.5 x 20cm (5¾ x 8in) of white 14-count Aida fabric
- One skein of stranded cotton in each colour listed in the key
- Size 26 tapestry needle
- Red card with rectangular opening measuring 11 x 15cm (4¼ x 6in)

Note
Although this Santa makes a good card it could equally well be framed and kept as a Christmas keepsake which could be brought out each year. On the chart, note that white cross stitch is outlined to show where it finishes. Do not work this as back stitch.

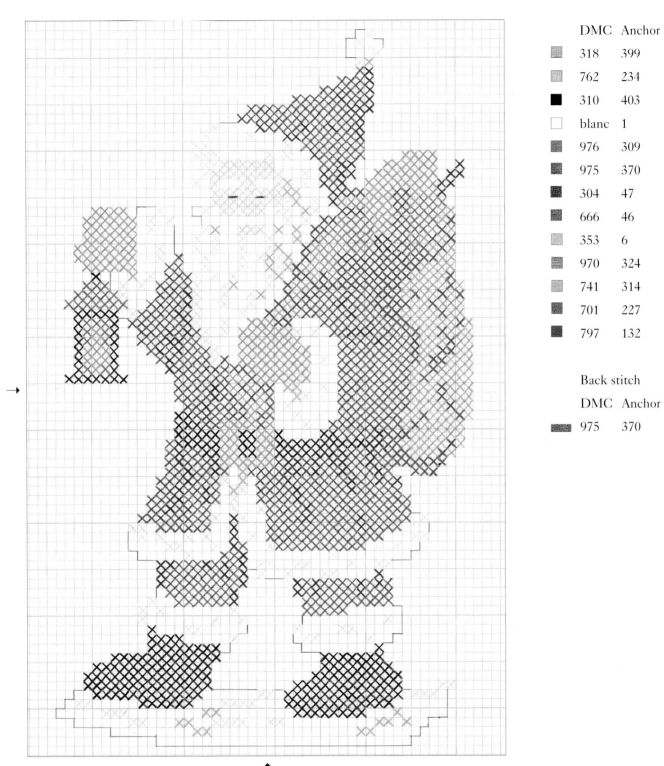

DMC Anchor
318 399
762 234
310 403
blanc 1
976 309
975 370
304 47
666 46
353 6
970 324
741 314
701 227
797 132

Back stitch
DMC Anchor
975 370

Poinsettia

The poinsettia epitomizes the spirit of Christmas. With its bright red flowers and deep green leaves you can't go wrong.

Measurements
The actual cross stitch design measures 6.8 x 6.8cm (2¾ x 2¾in)

Materials
- 13cm (5in) square of white 18-count Aida fabric
- One skein of stranded cotton in each colour listed in the key
- Size 26 tapestry needle
- Purple card with 8cm (3⅛in) diameter circular opening

DMC	Anchor		Back stitch	
816	1005		DMC	Anchor
347	13		938	381
351	10			
907	255		French knots	
3348	253		DMC	Anchor
			972	298

Holly and Ivy

Christmas wouldn't be Christmas without a touch of holly and ivy. Deck your mantel with this festive card.

Measurements
The actual cross stitch design measures 5.4 x 6.5cm (2⅛ x 2⅝in)

Materials
- 13cm (5in) square of white 18-count Aida fabric
- One skein of stranded cotton in each colour listed in the key
- Size 26 tapestry needle
- Green card with rectangular opening measuring 6.8 x 8cm (2¾ x 3⅛in)

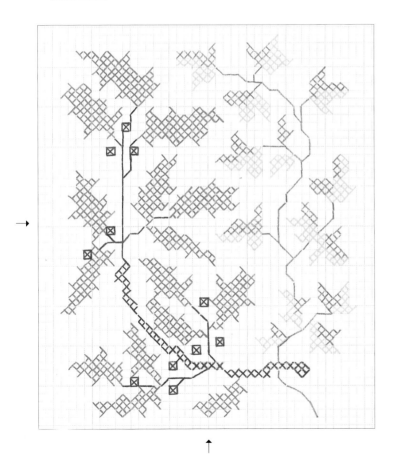

DMC	Anchor		Back stitch		
1 strand			DMC	Anchor	
469	267		469	267	ivy stems
472	278		319	217	holly stems
817	19				
319	217				
699	229				

Note
Why not try using red seed beads for the berries in this card? It is an unusual and very effective touch.

Robin

There's nothing more endearing than seeing a robin looking for scraps in the snow.
Don't you just want to take him home and look after him!

Measurements

The actual cross stitch design measures 12.7 x 7.5cm (4⅞ x 3in)

Materials

• 20 x 14.5cm (8 x 5¾ in) of white 14-count Aida fabric

• One skein of stranded cotton in each colour listed in the key

• Size 26 tapestry needle

• Dark green card with oval opening measuring 14.5 x 9.5cm (5¾ x 3¾ in)

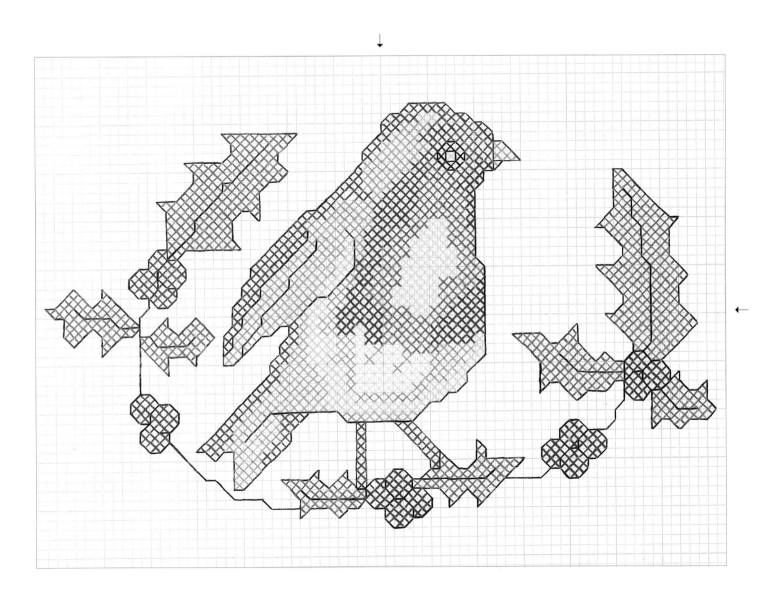

	DMC	Anchor		DMC	Anchor		DMC	Anchor	Back stitch		
	3362	263		739	366		225	892	DMC	Anchor	
	310	403		ecru	387		666	46	310	403	
	801	359		415	398						
	435	369		304	47						

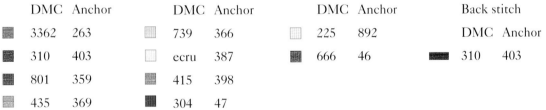

Winter Scene

*A snow-covered landscape looks beautiful.
Picture snow-peaked roofs to conjure up an
idyllic image of crisp winter days.*

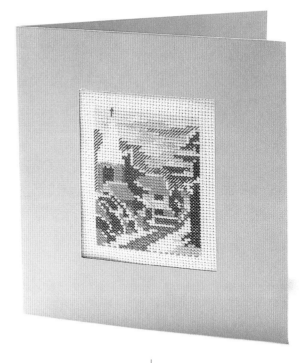

Measurements

The actual cross stitch design measures 5.5 x 6.8cm (2⅛ x 2¾in)

Materials

- 13cm (5in) square of white 18-count Aida fabric
- One skein of stranded cotton in each colour listed in the key
- Kreinik blending filament
- Size 26 tapestry needle
- Lavender card with rectangular opening measuring 6.8 x 8cm (2¾ x 3⅛in)

	DMC	Anchor
	3689	73
	3350	77
	210	109
	208	111
	794	120
	797	132
	742	303
	300	357
	613	853
	3011	856
	503	876
	699	923
	501	878

Half cross stitch

1 strand

	DMC	Anchor
	3354	74
	3350	77
	794	120
	797	132

Back stitch

	DMC	Anchor	
	300	357	church cross

Kreinik metallic

sky blue (014) lower line, icicle and
snow details

Fireplace and Stockings

...and while you're waiting for Santa to come and fill your stocking, you could cuddle up in front of a warm, glowing, cheery fire.

Measurements

The actual cross stitch design measures 4.6 x 6.6cm (1¾ x 2⅝in)

Materials

- 13cm (5in) square of white 18-count Aida fabric
- One skein of stranded cotton in each colour listed in the key
- Size 26 tapestry needle
- Red card with rectangular opening measuring 5.7 x 7.5cm (2¼in x 3in)

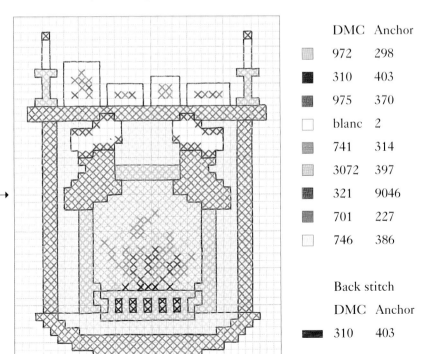

	DMC	Anchor
	972	298
	310	403
	975	370
	blanc	2
	741	314
	3072	397
	321	9046
	701	227
	746	386

Back stitch

	DMC	Anchor
	310	403

Note

Small ends of Kreinik thread worked into the flames of the fire will give them life and add a crackle and sparkle to this design.

Children's Toys

Remember when you were young? How pleased would you have been to receive a card like this? Or better still the toys themselves!

Measurements
The actual cross stitch design measures 12.5 x 8.3cm (4¾ x 3¼in)

Materials
• 14.5 x 20cm (5¾ x 8in) of white 14-count Aida fabric
• One skein of stranded cotton in each colour listed in the key
• Size 26 tapestry needle

• Yellow card with rectangular opening measuring 14.3 x 10.5cm (5⅝ x 4⅛in)

Note
If you've untold patience and want a truly awesome project, why not repeat this design to make a stunning fabric shelf border for a child's room? For a larger project still, you could use it as the mainstay of a room design.

	DMC	Anchor		DMC	Anchor	Back stitch
■	310	403		776	24	1 strand
□	blanc	1		677	300	DMC Anchor
	726	297	▦	3607	87	317 400 waistcoat outline, bricks, doll, soldier, balloon and
	225	892	▦	334	977	bow tie
	224	894		471	265	433 357 bear's outline, bear's cheeks and tummy button
	445	288	▦	413	401	
▦	321	9046				
	3072	397				Back stitch
	402	347		French knots		2 strands
	701	245		DMC	Anchor	DMC Anchor
	797	132	•••	317	400	310 403 bear's muzzle, numbers
						321 9046 waistcoat detail

Roses

If you're an ambitious stitcher this card will provide an ideal challenge. Beautiful big blooms will be a delight to stitch and a joy to receive.

Measurements
The actual cross stitch design measures
21 x 12.5cm (8¼ x 5in)

Materials
- 32 x 25cm (12 x 10in) of antique white
  27-count evenweave fabric
- One skein of stranded cotton in each colour
  listed in the key
- Size 26 tapestry needle
- Burgundy card with oval opening measuring
  22 x 15cm (8⅝ x 5⅞in)

Note
When working a large design like this one, you might find it easier to keep your place on your chart by using a sticky note which you can move around as you complete each bit.

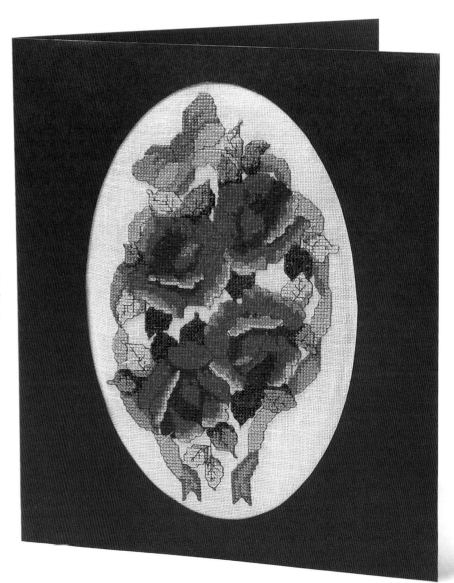

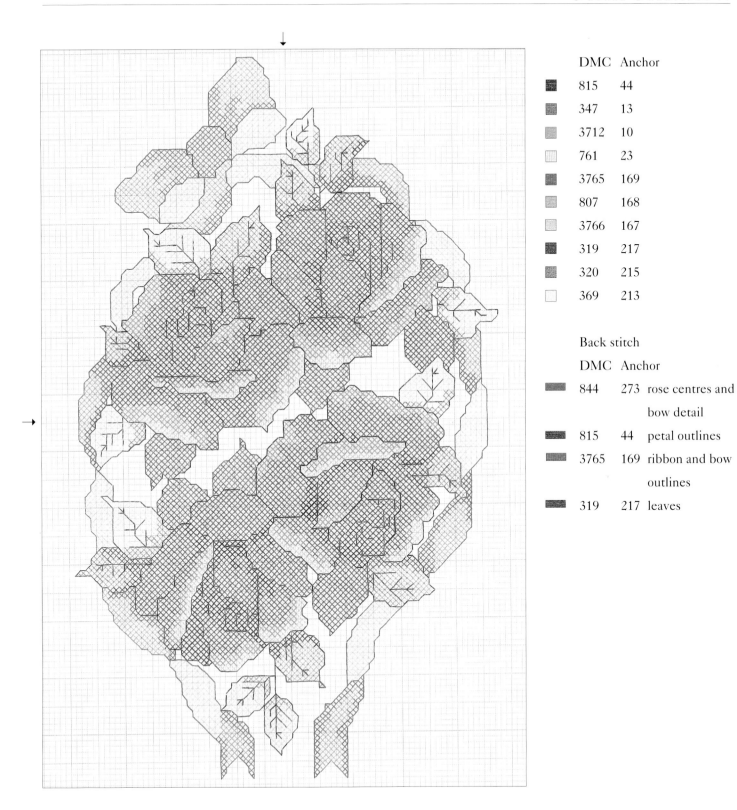

DMC Anchor

815 44

347 13

3712 10

761 23

3765 169

807 168

3766 167

319 217

320 215

369 213

Back stitch

DMC Anchor

844 273 rose centres and
bow detail

815 44 petal outlines

3765 169 ribbon and bow
outlines

319 217 leaves

Forget-me-nots

Designs don't need to be complicated to be good. This simple design could be stitched and sent in an hour. How's that for made to order?

Measurements

The actual cross stitch design measures 6.8 x 4.8cm (2¾ x 1⅞in)

Materials

- 13cm (5in) square of white 14-count Aida fabric
- One skein of stranded cotton in each colour listed in the key
- Size 26 tapestry needle
- Lilac card with oval opening measuring 7.5 x 5.5cm (3 x 2⅛in)

	DMC	Anchor		Back stitch	
				DMC	Anchor
	307	289			
	367	216		890	683
	793	176			
	792	177			

Note

Omit the central floral motif and stitch your own special greeting on this card using letters from one of the alphabets which begin on page 98.

Honeysuckle

This design is so life-like you can almost smell the sweet scent of the delicate flowers.

Measurements

The actual cross stitch design measures 7 x 7.5cm (2¾ x 3in)

Materials

- 13cm (5in) square of white 18-count Aida fabric
- One skein of stranded cotton in each colour listed in the key
- Size 26 tapestry needle
- Yellow card with oval opening measuring 8 x 8.5cm (3⅛ x 3⅜in)

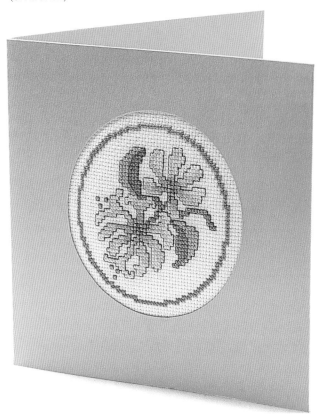

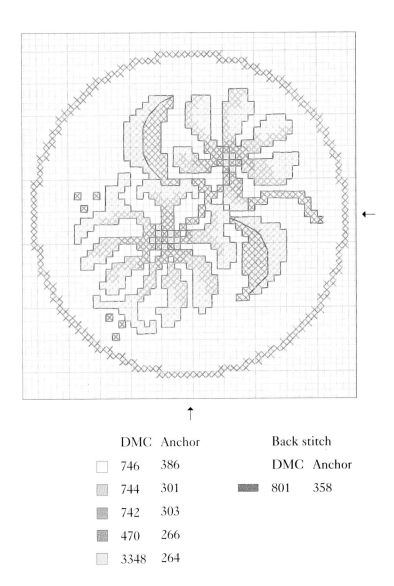

DMC	Anchor		Back stitch	
746	386		DMC	Anchor
744	301		801	358
742	303			
470	266			
3348	264			

Note

If you have to unpick your work for any reason and find yourself with bits of fluff, roll them off by wrapping sticky tape around a cotton bud and dabbing it around the fluffy bits of thread.

Arum Lilies

Tall, lean, elegant and pure, that's a common perception of the lily. What a lovely perception to have of someone special. Let them know by sending them this card.

Measurements

The actual cross stitch design measures 9 x 12.8cm (3½ x 5in)

Materials

- 14.5 x 20cm (5¾ x 8in) of white 14-count Aida fabric
- One skein of stranded cotton in each colour listed in the key
- Size 26 tapestry needle
- Cream card with rectangular opening measuring 10.5 x 14cm (4⅛ x 5½in)

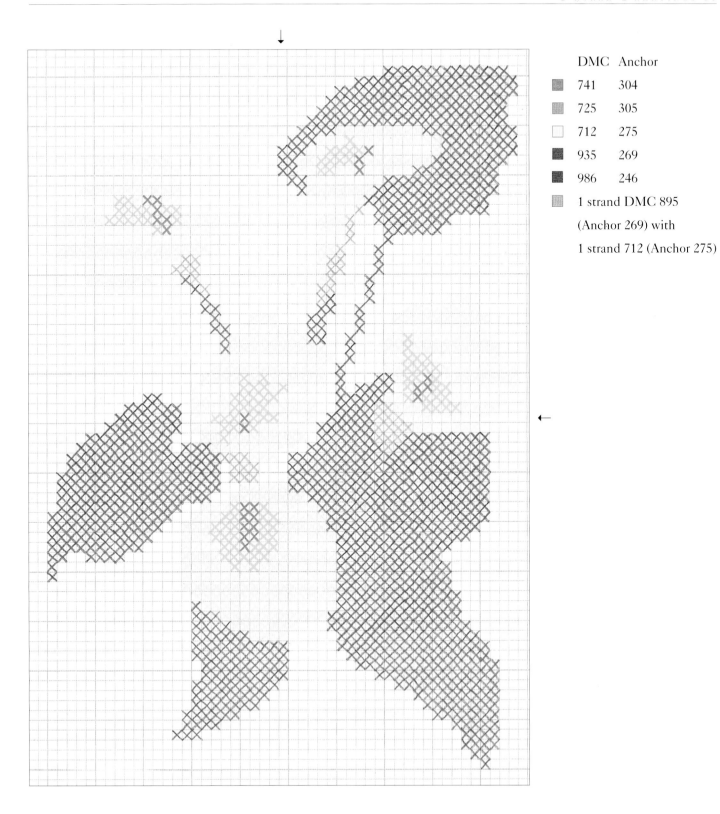

DMC	Anchor
741	304
725	305
712	275
935	269
986	246

1 strand DMC 895
(Anchor 269) with
1 strand 712 (Anchor 275)

Poppies

Cheerful poppies make a striking greeting ideal for livening up someone's special day.
This easy-to-stitch design can be worked by even the most novice stitcher.

Measurements
The actual cross stitch design measures 3.6 x 7cm
(1⅜ x 2¾in)

Materials
• 13cm (5in) square of white 14-count Aida fabric

• One skein of stranded cotton in each colour
  listed in the key
• Size 26 tapestry needle
• Mauve card with oval opening measuring
  5 x 7.5cm (2 x 3in)

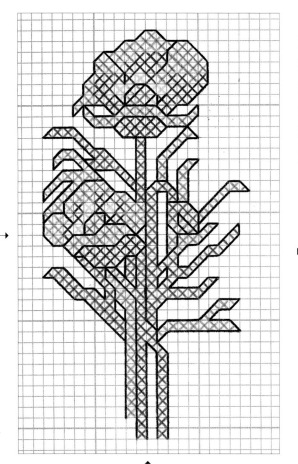

DMC	Anchor
817	19
350	11
701	227
702	226
3799	236
307	289

Backstitch

DMC	Anchor
310	403

Bluebells

The bluebell is one of spring's most beautiful gems. When you see its rich blue flower you know it's a harbinger of the coming summer.

Measurements

The actual cross stitch design measures 4.8 x 7.5cm (1⅞ x 3in)

Materials

- 13cm (5in) square of white 18-count Aida fabric
- One skein of stranded cotton in each colour listed in the key
- Size 26 tapestry needle
- Bright green card with rectangular opening measuring 6 x 8cm (2⅜ x 3⅛in)

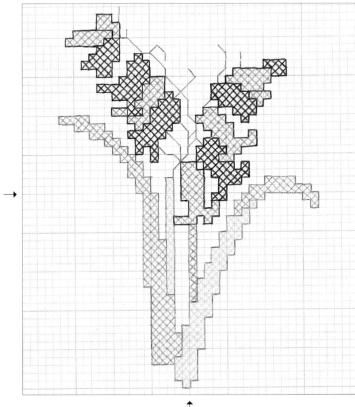

	DMC	Anchor		Back stitch		
				DMC	Anchor	
	793	118		333	119	
	333	119		3346	267	
	989	265				
	3346	267				

Daisies

Daisies may be simple flowers, but if you want to send a special message their simplicity makes them the perfect choice! Stitch them into a pretty chain.

Measurements
The actual cross stitch design measures 7.5 x 11cm (3 x 4⅜in)

Materials
- 14.5 x 20cm (5¾ x 8in) of cream 18-count Aida fabric
- One skein of stranded cotton in each colour listed in the key
- Size 26 tapestry needle
- Lilac card with oval opening measuring 9.5 x 13.5cm (3¾ x 5⅜in)

DMC   Anchor

1 strand

☐	blanc	1
▨	754	4146
▨	839	360
▨	444	291
▨	3348	264
▨	772	259
▨	841	378
▨	347	13
▨	351	10
▨	352	9

Back stitch

DMC   Anchor

▨	3346	267

French knots

2 strands

DMC   Anchor

○○○	blanc	1
●●●	839	360

Tulips

Reminiscent of the tulips on Dutch china, these stylized flowers are easy to stitch and quick to finish.

Measurements
The actual cross stitch design measures 4.8 x 7.2cm (1⅞ x 2⅞in)

Materials
- 13cm (5in) square of white 18-count Aida fabric
- One skein of stranded cotton in each colour listed in the key
- Size 26 tapestry needle
- Bright blue card with 8.3cm (3¼in) diameter circular opening

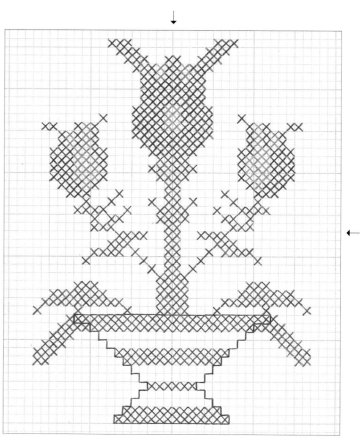

DMC	Anchor		Back stitch	
347	19		DMC	Anchor
3705	35		797	132
699	923			
797	132			

Sunflowers

For a special floral greeting, stitch these delicate sunflowers. Anyone receiving this card will be all sunny smiles.

Measurements

The actual cross stitch design measures 4.8 x 7cm (1⅞ x 2¾in)

Materials

- 13cm (5in) square of white 18-count Aida fabric
- One skein of stranded cotton in each colour listed in the key
- Size 26 tapestry needle
- Yellow card with oval opening measuring 5.2 x 8cm (2 x 3⅛in)

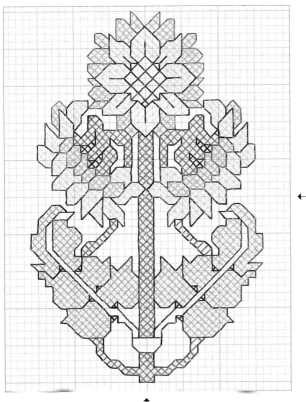

Note

If you use a larger count fabric, you can turn this lovely design into a bigger picture which could then be framed or worked as a front piece to a fabric bag.

	DMC	Anchor		Back stitch		
	1 strand			DMC	Anchor	
	677	300		433	371	top flower outline,
	726	295				inner detail of side flowers
	991	189		3371	382	leaves, stems,
	993	186				remainder of flowers
	3371	382				

DESIGN SOURCES

*Add a personal touch to your work by using these pages for inspiration. Once
you've found something you like, select your own colours to suit the design you'd
like to enhance. Or combine some of these ideas to create your own design.*

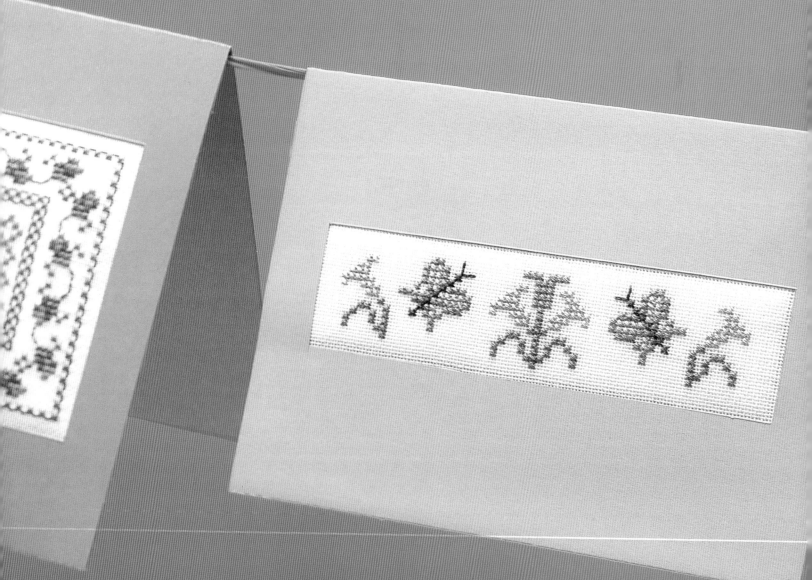

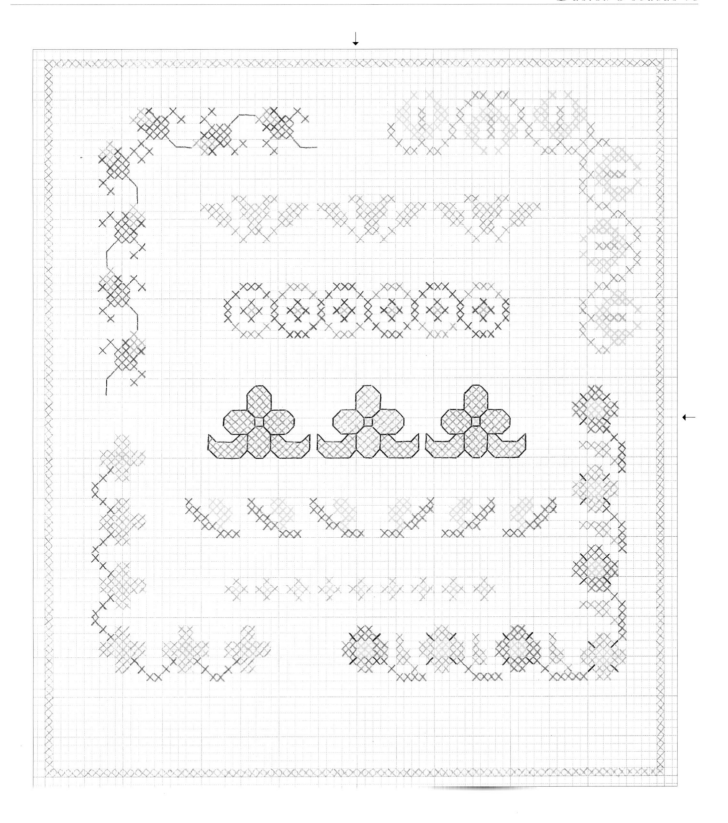

abcdefghijklm
nopqrstuvwxyz

ABCDE ЗGHIJKLM
NOPQRSTUVWXYZ

abcdefghijklmnopqrstuvwxyz

ABCDEFGHIJKLMNOPQRSTUVWXYZ

abcdefghijklm

nopqrstuvwxyz

ABCDEЗGHIJKLM

NOPQRSTUVWXYZ

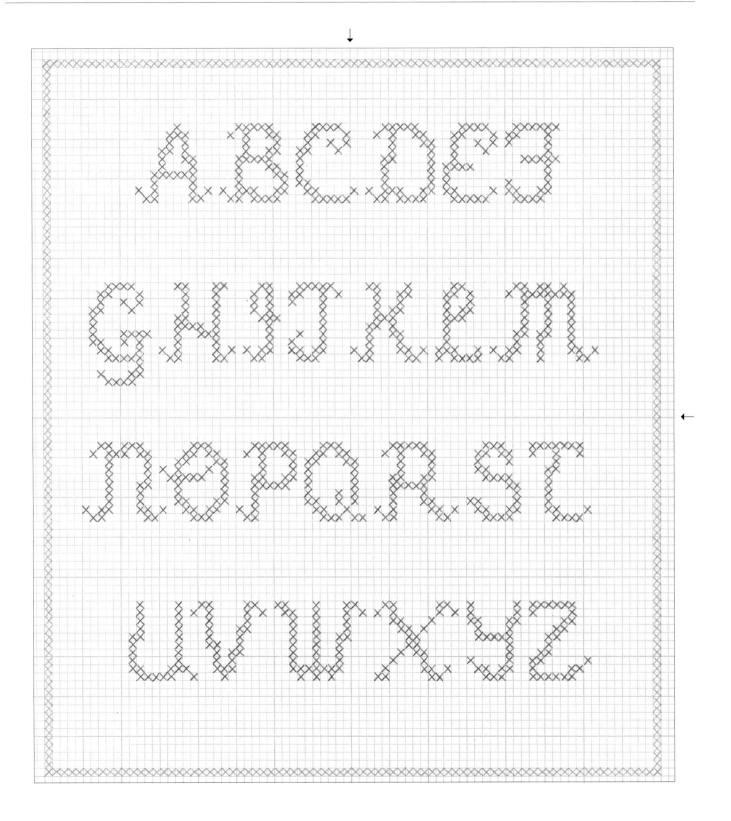

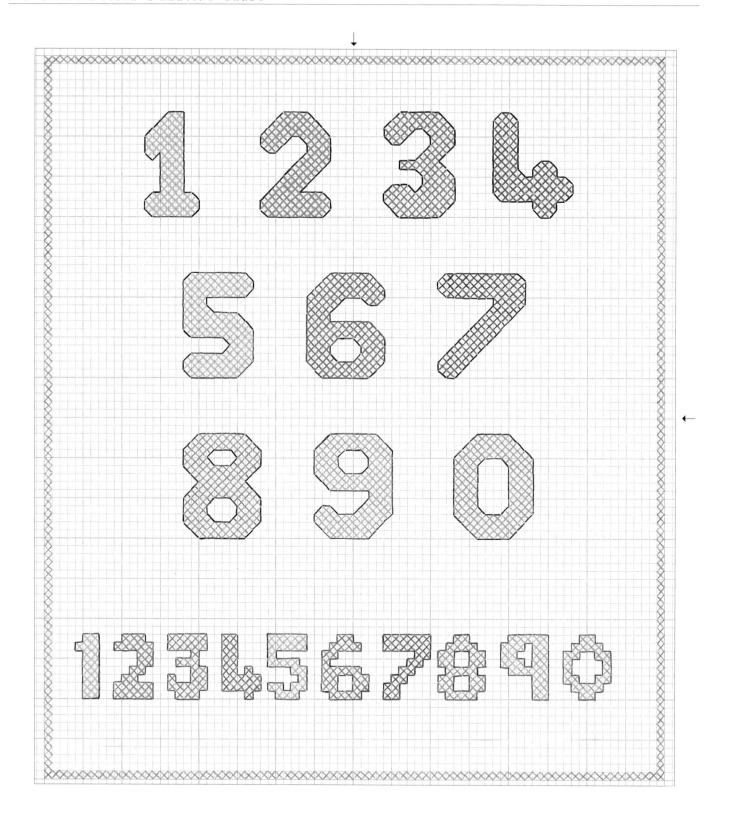

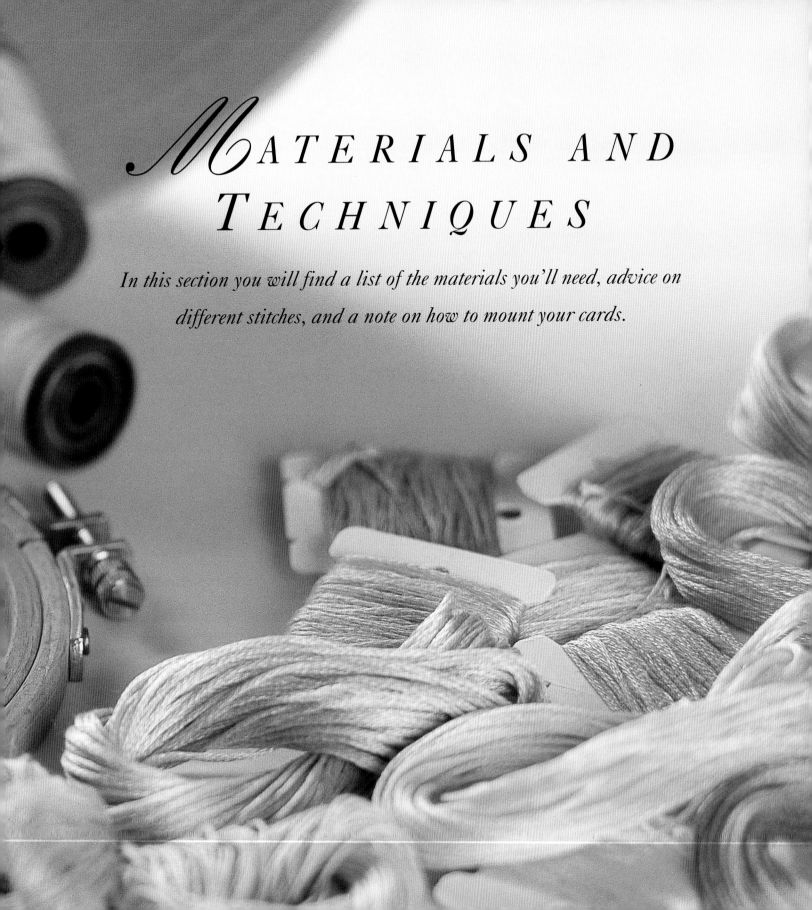

MATERIALS AND TECHNIQUES

In this section you will find a list of the materials you'll need, advice on different stitches, and a note on how to mount your cards.

Basic Equipment

Bobbins

Plastic or cardboard bobbins allow you to save unused strands of thread for re-use on a future project. Each will take a skein of thread and can be labelled with the thread make and number.

Card mounts

The card mounts used in this book show some of the wide range of sizes, shapes and colours available. All the cards used are known as double fold with aperture, meaning that each card is divided into three sections, with an aperture in the middle one. This enables you to mount your work with no raw edges showing and to have the back covered. Aperture shapes include rectangle, square, oval, circle and heart, and it is possible to obtain cards with an embossed, metallic or coloured line around the aperture. As with threads and fabrics, good embroidery shops should have a range of card mounts, but mail order is the best way to obtain the more unusual finishes or shapes (see page 111 for a suggested supplier).

Craft knife

A sharp knife is essential for obtaining a smooth, straight cut on card or paper. Replacement blades can be purchased separately.

Daylight simulation bulbs

These can be used in an anglepoise lamp for evening work, and for differentiating between similarly coloured threads.

Double-sided tape

This is good for mounting cards, being cleaner and easier to control than glue, which can be used if preferred.

Embroidery hoops and frames

The choice of a hoop or hand-held or floor-standing frame is a matter of personal preference. The use of either reduces distortion of your fabric, and it is worth having several in different sizes. It is a good idea to bind the inner hoop with tape or bias cut fabric to prevent it from marking your fabric.

Fabrics

The popularity of cross stitch has led to a huge increase in the variety of fabrics available. Colours range from white and pastels to black, in fancy weaves, which include lurex threads, or rustic-style fabrics, and there are tablecloths, tea towels and baby afghans which incorporate embroidery fabric panels. However, there are two basic types of fabric: blockweave and evenweave.

Blockweave The most popular blockweave is Aida. As the name implies, this is woven in blocks, and stitches are worked in every hole. Aida is available in a variety of counts, which refers to the number of holes (and therefore stitches) per inch. The most common counts are 11, 14 and 18. The higher the count, the smaller the finished design. As well as standard Aida, it is now possible to buy Aida Plus, which has been specially treated to prevent fraying and is therefore ideally suited for projects such as bookmarks, tree decorations and three-dimensional designs. Aida band is also available in a variety of widths and counts, and is ideal for bookmarks, cakebands and for stitching onto items such as tea towels, bedlinen and curtains.

Evenweave This fabric has the same numbers of threads across and down, and, like Aida, is available in a range of widths and stitch counts. The most popular is 27/28 holes per inch. On evenweave, stitches are usually worked into every other hole; thus a 27/28-count evenweave will produce the same finished design size as a 14-count Aida. It may be made of pure linen, linen and cotton mixes, or pure cotton. Whilst it can be more difficult to count on evenweave than on Aida, it does come into its own with designs using fractional stitches. It is also possible to work over just one thread to produce a half-size design.

Iron-on interfacing

Lightweight iron-on interfacing (Vilene) is useful when mounting cross stitch in commercially available boxes.

Magnifying glass

Hung around your neck, this can help on higher count fabrics. Magnifying aids are also available for placing on charts.

Needles

Tapestry needles are ideal for cross stitch: they are blunt, so do not damage fabric, and have a relatively large eye, making them easy to thread. Sizes 24 and 26 are the most commonly used, the latter being the finer and suitable for either 14 or 18 holes per inch fabric. Use size 24 for 14-count. If you intend to use beads, you may also need beading (or 'straw') needles. These are very fine, with an eye barely thicker than the shaft of the needle.

Pencil and pen

A pencil can be used for marking fabric but it may not always wash out, so be careful not to use it where it will show. Fabric markers are available which will wash out. Highlighter pens can be useful for marking off the worked sections of a chart.

Pins

Stainless steel pins are the best since they will not rust and mark your fabric. Other types, such as gold-plated and glass-headed, are also available.

Ruler

A metal ruler has the advantage over a bevelled plastic ruler of providing a flat edge when cutting card or paper.

Scissors

A large pair of dressmaking scissors is essential, and a cheaper pair for paper and card. (Do not be tempted to use dressmaking scissors for cutting card – you will blunt them.) Embroidery scissors have small, pointed blades which are ideal for cutting threads close to your work and for unpicking, but take care not to poke the blades into the fabric. Or use a pair of snips. They consist of two blades held together by a wire spring.

Tailor's chalk

Used for marking fabric, this will brush or wash away. It comes in a variety of colours to show up on different coloured fabrics.

Tape measure

It is best to choose a plastic-coated tape measure with both metric and imperial markings. It will not stretch out of shape in the way that a cloth one does and so it will give more accurate measurements.

Thimble

Use a thimble if you like. It's a matter of personal preference.

Threads

Again, the growth in the popularity of cross stitch has resulted in a broader range of threads. Most can be obtained from good embroidery shops, but mail order is also available.

Stranded cotton The projects in this book use stranded cotton, which comes in an excellent range of colours. The cotton has six strands which can be separated to produce the required number for a design. A design with 14 stitches per inch generally uses two strands, but a more intense effect can be obtained by using three strands. With 18 stitches per inch, two strands will produce a more solid effect, whereas one strand will give a lighter effect. In this book, there are usually two strands for cross stitch and one strand for back stitch and French knots unless otherwise stated.

Flower threads These are available in a narrower range of colours than stranded cottons and are single strands which should not be divided before using. They give a matt effect.

Marlitt This is lustrous and gives a sheen to your work. The colour range is more limited than that for stranded cottons.

Metallic threads These are available in a wide variety of colours and thicknesses. The finest is blending filament, which can be used on its own, single or double, or can be blended with one strand of stranded cotton. Two strands of blending filament is equivalent to two strands of embroidery cotton. The effect adds lustre and depth. Thicker metallic threads can be used singly as an alternative to stranded cotton – different thicknesses suit different gauges of fabric.

Tweezers

These are useful for removing threads when unpicking, and for removing the backing paper from double-sided tape.

Wadding (batting)

If you place a piece of lightweight wadding (2oz) behind your design when you mount it in a card, you will achieve a more professional, three-dimensional finish.

Mounting the Cards

You will need:

- card with suitable aperture
- stitched piece
- double-sided tape
- 2oz wadding (batting)
- all-purpose scissors
- pencil
- tweezers

1 Fold the card along the scored foldlines if this has not already been done. Open it out and place the card right-side down on a piece of wadding. Draw carefully around the aperture onto the wadding with a pencil, taking care not to mark the mount. Lift the card off and cut along the pencil line.

2 Place the opened card right-side down on a clean surface. Cut some pieces of double-sided tape and stick them all around the aperture. Then remove the backing paper from the tape, using tweezers to lift the backing paper if you have difficulty.

3 Place the embroidery right-side up on your work surface and gradually lower the card mount onto it, right-side up. Ensure your design is straight and central in the aperture. When you are happy with the positioning, press down carefully to stick your embroidery to the tape. Ensure that the embroidery remains taut.

4 Turn the card over. Place your wadding over the back of your cross stitch and secure with tape.

5 Stick double-sided tape to the side of the card which will cover the back of the embroidery. This is the left-hand panel on a side-opening card and the top panel on a bottom-opening card. Remove backing paper and press card shut firmly. With your finger, rub along the edges of the card and around the aperture to ensure adhesion.

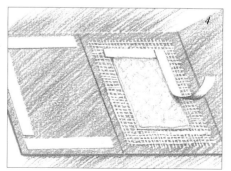

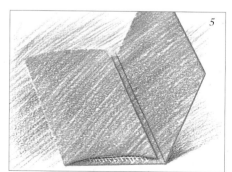

Make sure you keep your stitched work taut when you position it on the tape behind the card's aperture.

Suppliers

UK

Coats Crafts UK
PO Box 22, The Lingfield Estate
McMullen Road
Darlington
County Durham DL1 1YQ
Tel : 01325 394394
(Suppliers of embroidery fabrics, Anchor threads and Kreinik metallic threads)

Craft Creations Ltd
Units 1-7
Harper's Yard
Ruskin Road
Tottenham
London N17 8QA
Tel : 0181 885 2655
Fax : 0181 808 0746
(Suppliers of card mounts, card, paper, packaging, picture mounts, etc. Orders accepted from abroad)

DMC Creative World
Pullman Road
Wigston
Leicester
Leicestershire   E18 2DY

USA

The DMC Corporation
Port Kearny
Building 10
South Kearny
New Jersey 070032

Coats and Clark
Greenville
South Carolina
(Anchor threads)

Joan Toggit Ltd
2 Riverview Drive
Somerset
New Jersey 08873
(Zweigart fabrics)

AUSTRALIA AND NEW ZEALAND

DMC
51-61 Carrington Road
Marrickville
New South Wales 2204

Warnaar Trading Co Ltd
376 Ferry Road
PO Box 19567
Christchurch
(DMC threads and Zweigart fabrics)

Coats Patons Crafts
Mulgrave 3170
Australia
(Anchor threads)

SOUTH AFRICA

SATC
43 Somerset Road
PO Box 3868
Capetown 800
(DMC threads)

Brasch Hobby
10 Loveday Street
PO Box 6405
Johannesburg 2000
(Zweigart fabrics)

NEEDLE PRODUCTS

All DMC and Anchor threads and Zweigart fabrics used in this book are available from the relevant stockists given below and many other needlecraft outlets the world over. The addresses given are the head offices or agents – contact them for advice on local availability of threads. Good haberdasheries should also supply other products, including embroidery hoops, cards, needles, scissors etc.

Index

ACKNOWLEDGEMENTS

The authors would like to thank the following designers for use of their designs:

LYNDA BURGESS – 18/21 flower/key, 18/21 wild rose, forget-me-nots, poppies;

LESLEY GRANT – Moses basket, 18/21 motorbike, 70/80/90 female, exams, New Year chimney sweep, Father's day (man and dog in pub), winter scene, sunflower, wedding doves (card and tag);

LUCIE HEATON – animal sampler, bear repeat, toy sampler, New Year champagne;

STEVEN JENKINS – 18/21 football, 70/80/90 male, Mother's day bouquet, holly and ivy;

PENELOPE RANDALL – boy's 1st birthday, girl's 1st birthday, new job, travel, Santa;

JANE RIMMER – good luck, driving test (car), Easter chick, robin;

JULIA TIDMARSH – stork (card and tag), engagement congratulations, new home, Easter cross, Valentine's day, poinsettia, fireplace with stockings, honeysuckle, daisies;

SUE WHITING – bride and groom, silver anniversary, arum liles, bluebells, tulips;

LYNDA WHITTLE – rabbit in hospital bed, get well soon flower basket, wedding sampler, presents with doll/teddy, roses.

Special thanks also to Coats Crafts UK and to Craft Creations Ltd for providing materials for the cards.